THE POWER OF A PARENT'S WORDS

In appreciation for your support of Focus on the Family, please accept this copy of *The Power of a Parent's Words* by Norm Wright. Your contributions enable this organization to address the needs of homes through radio, television, literature and counseling.

We trust you'll be encouraged by the practical parenting advice on the following pages, and we hope you agree that it will make a fine addition to your family's library.

Focus on the Family
Pomona, CA 91799

From the Author of the #1 Best-seller *Always Daddy's Girl*

THE POWER OF A PARENT'S WORDS

How You Can Use Loving, Effective
Communication to Increase Your Child's Self-Esteem
and Reduce the Frustrations of Parenting

H. Norman Wright

Regal Books

A Division of GL Publications
Ventura, California, U.S.A.

Published by Regal Books
A Division of GL Publications
Ventura, California 93006
Printed in U.S.A.

Library of Congress Cataloging-in-Publication Data

Wright, H. Norman.
    The power of a parent's words: how you can use loving, effective communication to increase your child's self-esteem and reduce the frustrations of parenting / H. Norman Wright.
      p. cm.
    Includes bibliographical references.
    ISBN 0-8307-1493-6
    1. Parenting—United States. 2. Communication in the family—United States. I. Title.
HQ755.8.W73 1991
306.874—dc20
                                        90-22001
                                           CIP

Any omission of credits is unintentional. The publisher requests documentation for future printings.

Rights for publishing this book in other languages are contracted by Gospel Literature International (GLINT) foundation. GLINT also provides technical help for the adaptation, translation, and publishing of Bible study resources and books in scores of languages worldwide. For further information, contact GLINT, Post Office Box 488, Rosemead, California, 91770, U.S.A., or the publisher.

CONTENTS

Introduction 9

Are You a Frustrated Parent?

PART I:
THE NURTURING PARENT

1. Do You Have a Healthy, Communicating Family? 17

"The atmosphere of the home, including verbal and nonverbal communication from parents, plays a significant role in shaping a child's identity and behavior."

2. Why Did You Become a Parent? 35

"Our goal as parents is to empower our children to become mature and to release them to become independent from us and dependent on God."

3. Parental Roles and Character Goals 51

"One of our great challenges and delights is to honor our child's uniqueness and accept what cannot be changed in him."

4. Are You Parenting Without a Compass? 65

"The sooner you recognize that you are not headed in the direction you want to go, the easier it
will be to get back on course."

5. The Myths of Parenting 77

"If we don't change some of our false beliefs about
parenting, we will stagnate and lock ourselves and
our families into untruth."

PART II:
POLLUTION-FREE COMMUNICATION

6. Let's Ban the Toxic Verbal Weapons 95

"Our words are often launched as verbal missiles to
attack a child's behavior, appearance, intelligence,
competence or value as a person."

7. How to Frustration-proof Your Communication 115

"If you deal with your frustration before it ignites
into anger, you can keep yourself from exploding
with hurtful words."

8. Messages that Discount, Messages that Nurture 135

"Nurturing messages increase your child's value in
his own eyes, thus opening the door for learning,
growth, maturity and independence."

PART III:
TAILOR-MADE COMMUNICATION TO FIT YOUR CHILD

9. Every Child Is a Priceless Original 155

"In order to understand your children better, appreciate them more and communicate with them
effectively, it is very important that you discover
each child's uniqueness."

10. Getting Through to Number One   171

"Eager first-time parents want to parent better than anyone ever did before, and so the first-born becomes the victim of their inexperience, high hopes and enthusiasm."

11. Communicating with the Rest of the Tribe   185

"Once you get a handle on each child's unique birth-order traits, you will find it easier to keep family relationships operating smoothly."

12. You've Got Personality, Part One   203

"The key to reducing your frustration over your child's quirks of behavior is to understand and accommodate his personality style."

13. You've Got Personality, Part Two   223

"The more you understand the combinations of personality preferences in your children, the better prepared you will be to nurture them."

Conclusion: A Brief Review   247

"You have the opportunity to grow, change and learn to enjoy and nurture your child."

Introduction

ARE YOU A FRUSTRATED PARENT?

NORMA stepped quickly out of her 12-year-old daughter's bedroom and closed the door behind her. She was somewhat pleased with herself for not stomping out angrily and slamming the door. That's what she felt like doing after her confrontation with Alicia. And lately it seemed that most of Norma's interactions with Alicia ended up in a confrontation— usually over the biggest sore spot between them: Alicia's procrastination with school work.

"I can't believe she's done it again," Norma muttered to herself as she hurried downstairs to the kitchen. "I've told her time and time again to get her oral reports for school prepared early. But she always puts them off until the last minute. And she wasn't even going to tell me about the report she's supposed to give tomorrow! If I hadn't asked her about it, she would have made some lame excuse to her teacher and taken a failing grade on the project. I wouldn't have heard about it until the next parent-teacher conference. Sometimes that girl makes me so mad!"

With Alicia confined to her room until supper, Norma picked up the cordless kitchen phone to call her friend from church, Bernadette, and vent her frustration. She switched the phone on, but before she could push the first number, Norma heard Alicia's voice in the receiver. She was on the extension Norma had installed in her room so she could talk to her friends about homework. Norma usually replaced the receiver immediately when her daughter was on the line. But this time the receiver seemed frozen to her ear. Alicia was crying. Norma held her breath and listened.

"My mother just doesn't understand how hard it is for me to talk in front of class," Alicia sobbed.

"I know," her friend and classmate Tina consoled, trying to sound like a big sister. "Our mothers all think they understand us, but they really don't."

"She always says, 'You can do it, Alicia. After all, public speaking was my best subject in school. All you have to do is try harder. You're just procrastinating.' She calls me 'lazy' and quotes verses from the Bible about how important it is to work hard and not be a sluggard—whatever that is. I want to make Mom happy, but I just can't seem to please her. And when I tell her how hard it is for me to give oral reports, she just lectures me. She thinks she's helping me, but..."

Alicia's sentence was choked off by another sob. Norma silently switched off the phone and stared blankly at the kitchen cupboard. *I've really hurt her,* she thought in disbelief as a lump of emotion swelled in her throat. *I didn't know she was struggling so much with her school reports. I've been trying to encourage her and motivate her. Instead I've discouraged her and wounded her with my words. This is even more frustrating than Alicia's procrastination. I must stop hurting her and start nurturing her with my conversation. But I'm not sure how to do either.*

Does this scene seem strangely familiar? Perhaps the names and details are a little different, but you may be able to identify with the parental frustration Norma experienced over Alicia's apparent procrastination. Or maybe your frustration springs from other annoying traits and behaviors your child exhibits: He or she is loud, sloppy, rude to his siblings, careless, absentminded, lazy, picky . . . and the list goes on.

You may also empathize with this mother's sorrow because at times, in your frustration, you have wounded your child with your words. Your intentions were good; you wanted the best for him or her. But somehow you ended up communicating anger or disappointment instead of the encouragement your child needed. Perhaps your greatest frustration is reflected in Norma's final thought: You want to stop communicating words that wound and start communicating words that nurture, but you're not sure where to start.

I have talked to scores of frustrated parents like Norma in my counseling office and my seminars over the years. These good, loving Christian couples and single parents come to me and say, "Norm, we love our kids, and we want to raise them in the nurture and admonition of the Lord. But how can we live out this concern in our communication with our kids? What guidelines can you suggest that will help us learn to nurture them through what we say?" Maybe you've picked up this book because you are struggling with the same questions.

This book summarizes the communication guidelines I have shared with parents in my office and in my seminars across America. The chapters ahead will help you evaluate your present style of parenting and communicating with your children, identify negative traits which need to be changed and implement nurturing communication strategies that focus on each child's uniqueness. Every chapter concludes with exercises which will encourage you, your spouse and your study group (if you're working through this book with other parents) to apply these guidelines in your own homes.

In order to successfully implement these parent communication guidelines in your home, you need to understand where you're coming from as a parent. What is your present family like? What roles are being played out by your children? What was your family of origin like? What role did you play as a child? How did the communication style of your parents influence your communication style with your children? What motivated you to become a parent? Do you have an overall goal for your parenting? If so, is it a valid goal? Are dysfunctional traits in your family keeping you from reaching your goal? Is your parenting style based on the truth of Scripture or on the myths of parenting which are in circulation today? Part I of this book addresses these foundational issues.

We hear a lot about child abuse in society today. Many Christian parents feel they are completely innocent of this offense because they don't physically beat or sexually molest their children. But what about verbal abuse? Are you aware of the hurtful verbal missiles that we thoughtlessly launch at our children? Do you realize that we often allow frustration and anger to trigger words that wound our children more seriously than a bullet could? Can you distinguish between messages that discount your children and messages that nurture them? Part II identifies many of the forms of communication pollution which must be eradicated from parent-child interaction.

The more you understand your child's uniqueness, the better prepared you will be to nurture him with your words. Do you know what motivates each of your children? Have you discovered the inner clock by which each child operates in life? Are you aware of each child's unique learning style? Are you in tune with the unique blend of traits each child inherited through his genes, his birth order and his personality type? Part III will guide you in tailoring your parent-child communication to fit each uniquely original child in your home.

After Alicia had gone to bed Norma telephoned her friend Bernadette and tearfully recounted what she overheard on the kitchen phone that afternoon. Norma was surprised to learn that Bernadette had suffered through a similar crisis a few years earlier with her son Brad.

"I realized at that time that I was out of sync with who Brad was and what he needed from me," Bernadette confessed. "Instead of communicating with him in a nurturing way, in my frustration I just kept harassing him verbally trying to get him to do what he was supposed to do. I had no idea I was wounding him so deeply until his Sunday School teacher told me about a prayer request Brad verbalized in class: 'I want God to help Mommy not to be mad at me all the time.' That's when I knew I needed to do something about my style of communicating with Brad.

"Thank the Lord, Norma, I've changed. I really think I'm nurturing Brad with my words instead of wounding him. I'll be glad to share with you some of the things I've learned in the last couple of years."

Before the conversation was over, Norma and Bernadette had made plans to meet for lunch and talk about parent-child communication.

The three most helpful words I can share with you about your communication style with your children are these: *You can change!* You are not the hopeless, helpless victim of your parents' parenting style, your limited parent-child communication skills or your inexperience as a parent. There are good resources for growth and change available—you're holding one of them in your hands right now! It is possible to reduce your parenting frustration as you take positive steps toward change. May God use these pages to equip you for continued growth as a nurturing parent.

H. Norman Wright

Part I

THE NURTURING PARENT

1

DO YOU HAVE A HEALTHY, COMMUNICATING FAMILY?

SEVERAL of the young parents arrived early for the get-together at the home of Marv and Alma Johnston. The meeting was the result of a number of couples and single dads and moms in the church expressing a desire to compare notes on parenting. Most of them felt content and comfortable with how their children, ranging in age from 5 to 11, were progressing in life. There were no serious discipline or emotional problems among these kids. Yet a number of the adults who crowded into the Johnston's family room carried vague, unspoken concerns about their role as parents.

"This is an informal meeting," Marv said after a

word of prayer, "so we're going to share informally about our families. Let's take turns describing our children, our family life, and any problems we may be facing."

The group responded eagerly. As the parents spoke, the families they described seemed to reflect a cross-section of American family life. The problems they shared were mostly minor and fairly common. Still, many in the group hinted that their kids' behavior sometimes caused them to feel uncertain about their effectiveness in parenting.

A man sitting near the back of the room was the last parent to speak. "My name is Frank. Thank you for sharing so openly about your families. What I've heard here tonight is similar to what I've heard in other parent groups over the last few years. You know me as a parent, but you need to know something else about me which definitely relates to what we are discussing. I grew up in a dysfunctional family, and I'm still recovering from dysfunctional behavior patterns I inherited from that environment. I was abused as a child. No, I wasn't beaten, kicked, sexually molested or locked in a closet for days. The abuse I suffered was more subtle. It didn't inflict any physical wounds or leave visible scars. Yet I have come to learn that my abuse wounded and scarred me deeply inside. You see, I was verbally abused." Several parents stifled gasps of surprise as Frank continued.

"As I listened to you describe your families, some of your stories reminded me of my home. I heard you describe children who appear to be healthy but who in reality are showing early signs of dysfunctional behavior. Thankfully, physical and sexual abuse are not a problem in this group. But if you came from a home where verbal abuse was present, that tendency will probably be perpetuated in your own family."

Frank paused for a moment, and the silence was deafening. All eyes were glued on him. No one stirred. Many of the parents felt the uncomfortable weight of his words. Finally one of the mothers broke the silence. "Will you identify for us what you heard tonight that caused your concern? Most of us shared similar descriptions of our children and their behavior. Are we all on the wrong track?"

"I'm not saying that all our kids are going to end up as criminals or derelicts," Frank answered with a smile. "But the track many of us are on with our kids may not be headed toward the destination we have in mind for them. You see, the parenting track you follow is the result of your past experiences. The way you talk to your kids probably seems normal to you because that's the way you were talked to as a child. But what you accept as normal isn't necessarily right. To a large degree, the way we talk to our kids determines the role they play in the family and shapes the patterns of behavior and response they will carry into adulthood. That's why it's so important that we communicate with our children according to the guidelines given in God's Word."

TALKING CHILDREN INTO PLAYING A ROLE

"What do you mean by 'roles'?" asked a single parent of two. "Are you saying that some kids learn how to act a certain way in response to how we talk to them?"

"That's right," Frank said. "For some reason a child either develops a role in the family, or a role is consciously or unconsciously assigned to him by his parents. And this role becomes the child's identity. He learns how to survive in his family and gain a sense of self-worth by performing his role. The problem is that some elements of his true identity may be blocked by the role he has assumed. We know that a child's birth order, personality and unique make-up cause him to respond to life in a certain way. But he shouldn't be forced into that role or any other role. Balance and the ability to be flexible and experience different roles are what we are after.

"To illustrate what I mean by roles, let me play for you several segments of a cassette tape I brought along. The people you hear on the tape are parents like you and me describing their children as we did tonight. Would you like to hear some of them?" The group of parents enthusiastically voiced their interest, so Frank slipped the cassette into the Johnston's player and pushed START.

Jason the Doer

The first voice on the tape was that of a woman: "I can't believe the level of responsibility that our son Jason shows at age 10. Sometimes I wonder what we would do if it weren't for him. If my husband or I overlook any detail around the house, Jason is there to catch it for us. Sometimes he's like a little parent to his younger brother and sister. I think it's great, and Jason seems to thrive on doing things for us. In fact, I've seen him get upset if one of us takes care of something he thinks he can do. Perhaps he's just a typical first born. I'm glad he's happy. Other parents have told me they wish their kids were like Jason."

Frank stopped the tape. "Jason's role is that of a

doer. Somehow his parents have communicated to him that his worth and acceptance are based on his performance. Such children have an overly-developed sense of responsibility and struggle with guilt when they don't perform well. They don't really get much satisfaction out of all they do. Even as children they can become weary, feel taken advantage of and feel

---

In a healthy home, a child with doer tendencies is accepted even when he isn't doing something productive for the family. He is encouraged to develop balance between work and play in his life.

---

empty or neglected. That's the down side of being a doer. And when a child takes the role of a doer, he will grow up continuing in that role. Adult doers are often workaholics who must produce in order to feel worthwhile. Can any of you identify with the role of the doer?" A number of hands went up.

"In a dysfunctional home," Frank continued, "doers are rewarded and affirmed only when they perform. We all want our kids to be responsible. But some parents go too far and actually wound their children by saying things like, 'Mommy won't give you a hug until you've picked up your toys,' or 'If you can't sweep the porch better than that, you're no son of mine!' In a healthy home, a child with doer tendencies is accepted even when he isn't doing something productive for the family. He is encouraged to develop balance between work and play in his life."

Liz the Enabler

Frank started the tape again. The voice of another mother came through the speakers: "My daughter Liz is 13. I call her the stabilizer in our family. She keeps all of us on an even keel. I guess some people might say she's a peacemaker. I've even seen her take the blame for something her brother did just to avoid conflict in our home. Sometimes I wish she wouldn't do that, but I must admit that I enjoy the peace and quiet. Sometimes Liz can be so insistent about something that I call her a little nag. But she does it in a pleasant way."

Frank switched off the tape. "Children like Liz tend to take on the role of an enabler. They end up feeling responsible to provide the emotional nourishment for a family. They keep everyone together and smooth out the ruffled feathers. Somehow their parents communicated ideas like, 'God will punish you if you argue or fight' or 'If you kids don't get along, you're going to make Daddy and Mommy get a divorce.'

"Enablers live under the fear of abandonment. When they become adults they're afraid that other family members can't stand on their own two feet, so enablers feel duty-bound to help them survive."

A young mother a few chairs away from Frank sighed audibly. "You've just described me," she said. "Could enabling behaviors and responses actually keep some of the problems alive in a family? Sometimes I make excuses for others in my family, but they just continue in their problems."

"That's a good question and a good description," Frank replied. "In their efforts to solve problems and make peace, enablers often serve only to perpetuate the offensive and harmful behavior."

Jimmy the Loner

The next comment on the tape was from a father: "Sometimes I jokingly refer to my son as the invisible child. Jimmy moves through the house as quietly as a shadow, even when we have guests. He prefers to be alone, I guess, so perhaps he's just an introvert. Even when he comes and sits with us, he doesn't say too much. One thing I can say though: He's good and compliant, and I have yet to see him express any anger. That's a relief in light of what his older brother is like. Jimmy just kind of plods along steadily. He doesn't get much recognition at school or church, but that doesn't seem to bother him. He has a number of interests but seems to prefer being involved in these by himself."

"Invisible children like Jimmy can be called loners or lost children," Frank said as he stopped the tape. "Jimmy may appear well-behaved and compliant to his father, and who wouldn't like compliant children around? They give us some peace and quiet!" Several parents smiled and nodded. "But Jimmy is a lonely child because his parents have somehow conveyed that he's not very important. As a young child he was probably shushed when he made noise and shooed out of the room when he was a bother. His parents seemed to be happier when he wasn't around, so Jimmy adopted the loner's role. The Jimmys of the world grow up to be lost and lonely adults living in denial."

John the Star

Frank touched the START button again: "I'm so proud of John; he's such a talent in the family. He's gifted in so many areas and does most everything so well. And with him being such a stand out, we've become acquainted with so many neat people. Our life has changed a lot because of all John has accomplished. He really thrives on success and has such high standards, even though he tends to be a bit perfectionistic. Sometimes his sisters are bothered by his critical tendencies, but I think they could learn a lot about achieving from John."

Frank touched STOP. "Every parent wants his or her child to be a star or a hero, and we encourage our children to do the best they can according to their abilities. But like John's parents, some of us are so success-conscious for our kids that we push them too hard. They take on the role of the star and lose their childhood in the process. Their parents have instilled in them, 'Just making the team isn't good enough; you've got to be first-string and a league all-star,' or 'Dance lessons cost a lot of money, so you'd better get the lead role in every recital.' Stars are so busy achieving that they seldom take time just to have fun or do nothing for a while.

"It's all right for a child to not be the star. It's important for parents to affirm them verbally and nonverbally at all times for who they are. Children pushed into stardom by their parents often burn out, give up altogether and end up dismal failures as adults."

Amy the Joker

"You would love our daughter, Amy," the next mother on the tape said. "She's always the life of the party. She's so popular; everyone wants her around. She can be such a clown. She can make us laugh with her and at her. She's always joking and cutting up, even when she's facing a problem. Amy certainly knows how to enjoy life and help others enjoy life. Her attitude would go far toward helping other people."

"What's so bad about having a happy-go-lucky kid like Amy?" one of the parents asked as Frank stopped the tape.

"Nothing," Frank replied. "But when a joker like Amy finds it difficult to be serious at all, even when facing a problem or a tragedy, she's playing a role. She has received a message from her parents that her problems and pain are to be ignored, avoided or glossed over. Sometimes being the life of the party is a great cover-up for pain and isolation. We don't let people really know what's going on inside us. Unfortunately, some parents reinforce this behavior in their children and don't allow them to be serious. These kids learn that the only way to get attention is to be a joker.

"Are there any of you here tonight who wish others would take you more seriously and allow you to share your hurt?"

Several people raised a hand. Those sitting near them looked surprised, thinking their friends were just happy, jovial people without a real care in the world.

Eric the Saint

"May I play one more excerpt from the tape?" Frank asked. The group nodded.

A father's voice came through the speakers: "I think our Eric may grow up to be a minister. He's the good one in the family. We have such high hopes for him. He's so responsible and obedient. We've never had any problems with him. He's also very active in his youth group at church, and he encourages us to be consistent at church. At times he's like the family's conscience. Isn't that funny: a child calling us back to what we should be doing? He seems to carry us along. I think it's good that one of our kids is turning out this way."

"I think we all want our children to be good," Frank said as he switched off the cassette player and removed the tape. "But sometimes we hold unrealistic expectations for their behavior, and they adopt the role of the family saint trying to please us. Children playing this role often have areas in their lives which are deeply repressed or stunted. They avoid trying anything new for fear of failure." Many of the parents nodded knowingly.

Daddy's Little Princess and Mommy's Little Man

"There are a couple of nicknames that some parents use for their children which tend to push them into playing roles," Frank continued. "Have you ever heard a child called Daddy's Little Princess or Mommy's Little Man?" A number of heads in the group nodded. "Often these nicknames are used innocently and in fun, but in some families they are not harmless. Rather they are a subtle form of verbal abuse. For example, sometimes a father will push his daughter into the role of a little princess as a substitute for his wife in some ways. He may be afraid of seeking the fulfillment of his emotional needs from his wife, so he elevates his daughter to princess status and uses her to gain emotional fulfillment. This may make his daughter feel special at first, but she is denied her childhood because of the adult demands placed upon her. And yet she may enjoy the attention she receives and begin to demand it."

BAD NEWS AND GOOD NEWS ABOUT ROLES

One member of the group suggested that it was about time to adjourn the meeting. Marv Johnston agreed, then added, "This has been a wonderful meeting, and we're very grateful to you, Frank, for sharing with us what you've learned. Some of us are aware for the

> One of the most significant ways to help our children become functional adults is by learning to communicate with them in a positive way.

first time that we may also have been the victims of verbal abuse as children and that we have been abusing our children without knowing it. But it would be a shame to leave without some positive input on what to do with what we've heard. Do you have any good news for us, Frank?"

Frank smiled and nodded. "I realize that what I have said may cause you concern for yourself and your children. A large number of you have identified with these roles. Some of you are still living these roles. Perhaps you wish you could change. The good news is that you can!

"As for your children, you want each one of them to develop into a real person with a real identity and not take on a role to survive. The rest of the good news is that when you see negative tendencies occurring in your children, you can help them adjust and gain balance in their lives. One of the most significant ways to help our children become functional adults is by learning to communicate with them in a positive way. That's a big topic, but perhaps we can meet again and share some ideas. In the meantime, I suggest that you take some time to identify characteristics which might help you foster a healthy family atmosphere and positive communication with your children."

Before the group left the Johnston's they had scheduled a follow-up meeting in a week to discuss positive strategies for improving communication with their children.

Imagine that you had attended this meeting. What did you think about what Frank said? What feelings were aroused in you by his comments about verbal abuse? Can you identify family members in your past or present which fit his descriptions? How would you respond to Frank's assignment to identify the characteristics of a healthy family? At the close of this chapter you will have the opportunity to evaluate and discuss the presence of these roles in your family of origin and in your present family.

HEALTHY FAMILIES REQUIRE HEALTHY COMMUNICATION

A child's development is the result of many different factors in his life. He is the product of his birth order, his neurological structure, his interactions with other family members, his biological strengths and weaknesses, etc. But the atmosphere of the home, including verbal and nonverbal communication from parents, plays a significant role in shaping a child's identity and behavior.

The emotional life of a child actually begins at about the sixth month of his mother's pregnancy. In his book *The Secret Life of the Unborn Child,* Dr. Thomas Verny summarizes the current data on the impressionable nature of a fetus.

First, a fetus can hear, experience, taste and, on a very simple level, even learn and feel in utero.

Second, what a fetus feels and perceives begins to shape his attitudes and expectations about himself. These attitudes are developed from the messages he receives from his mother.

Third, the most significant factor in the fetus' emotional development is his mother's attitude. A mother with chronic anxiety or ambivalence about being a mother can leave an emotional scar on the unborn child's personality. On the other hand, joy, elation and anticipation can contribute significantly to the emotional development of a child.

Fourth, lest we leave out the father in this process, his feelings about his wife and unborn child are very important in determining the success of the pregnancy.[1]

Once a child is born he remains critically dependent on his parents for his emotional health and development. Consider for a moment the characteristics of a healthy or functional family. Notice how positive, nurturing communication is integral to the expression of each of these elements:

- The climate of the home is positive. The atmosphere is basically nonjudgmental.
- Each member of the family is valued and accept-

ed for who he or she is. There is regard for individual characteristics.

- Each person is allowed to operate within his or
  her proper role. A child is allowed to be a child
  and an adult is an adult.
- Members of the family care for one another, and
  they verbalize their caring and affirmation.
- The communication process is healthy, open and
  direct. There are no double messages.
- Children are raised in such a way that they can
  mature and become individuals in their own right.
  They separate from Mom and Dad in a healthy
  manner.
- The family enjoys being together. They do not get
  together out of a sense of obligation.
- Family members can laugh together, and they
  enjoy life together.
- Family members can share their hopes, dreams,
  fears and concerns with one another and still be
  accepted. A healthy level of intimacy exists within the home.

What about the home in which you were raised?
Do these characteristics describe your family of origin? Use the second exercise in the "For Thought and
Discussion" section below to rate each of the presence of each of the traits above in your family of origin and your present family. If your score for your
family of origin averages seven or above, you were
fortunate to be raised in a functional home. If your
score averages lower than seven, you may be the
product of a dysfunctional home. If so, there are several good books available which can help you deal
with your past in a positive way. If you are a woman,

I recommend *Always Daddy's Girl* (Regal Books), by this author. Another helpful book is *Pain and Pretending* (Thomas Nelson Publishers), by Rich Buhler.

If your score for your present family averages below seven, you may need to consider some course corrections. That's what this book is all about: helping you develop emotionally healthy, functional children through positive, nurturing communication. But before we get to specific communication strategies we need to look more closely at your goals as a parent, which is the focus of the next two chapters.

For Thought and Discussion

Share your responses with your spouse, a trusted friend or your study group.

1. Were any of the roles described in this chapter evident in your family of origin? Are any of them evident in your present family? If so, who played or plays these roles? Fill in the spaces below with the applicable names of the sibling(s) (don't forget yourself) in your family of origin and children in your present family.

- Who were/are the doers?
  Family of origin_____
  Present family _____

- Who were/are the enablers?
  Family of origin_____
  Present family _____

- Who were/are the loners?
  Family of origin_____
  Present family _____

- Who were/are the stars?
  Family of origin_____
  Present family _____

- Who were/are the jokers?
  Family of origin_____
  Present family _____

- Who were/are the saints?
  Family of origin_____
  Present family _____

- Who was Daddy's little princess and Mommy's little man?
  Family of origin_____
  Present family _____

2. On a scale of 0 (never evident) to 10 (always evident), rate the presence of the traits of a healthy family in your family of origin and present family.

- The climate of the home is positive.
  Family of origin   0 1 2 3 4 5 6 7 8 9 10
  Present family   0 1 2 3 4 5 6 7 8 9 10

- Each member of the family is valued and accepted for who he or she is.
  Family of origin   0 1 2 3 4 5 6 7 8 9 10
  Present family   0 1 2 3 4 5 6 7 8 9 10

- Each person is allowed to operate within his or her proper role.
  Family of origin   0 1 2 3 4 5 6 7 8 9 10
  Present family   0 1 2 3 4 5 6 7 8 9 10

- Members of the family care for one another, and they verbalize their caring and affirmation.

Family of origin   0 1 2 3 4 5 6 7 8 9 10
Present family   0 1 2 3 4 5 6 7 8 9 10

- Children are raised in such a way that they can mature and become individuals in their own right.
Family of origin   0 1 2 3 4 5 6 7 8 9 10
Present family   0 1 2 3 4 5 6 7 8 9 10

- The family enjoys being together.
Family of origin   0 1 2 3 4 5 6 7 8 9 10
Present family   0 1 2 3 4 5 6 7 8 9 10

- Family members can laugh together, and they enjoy life together.
Family of origin   0 1 2 3 4 5 6 7 8 9 10
Present family   0 1 2 3 4 5 6 7 8 9 10

- Family members can share their hopes, dreams, fears and concerns with one another and still be accepted.
Family of origin   0 1 2 3 4 5 6 7 8 9 10
Present family   0 1 2 3 4 5 6 7 8 9 10

Note

1. John Bradshaw, *Bradshaw on the Family* (Deerfield Beach, FL: Health Communications, Inc., 1988), adapted from the author's summary on pp. 26,27.

2

WHY DID YOU BECOME A PARENT?

THE three couples sat around a window table in the quiet, spacious restaurant. Each month they met here to enjoy a relaxing meal together without their 8 kids, ages 1 to 12. If the children had come with them, the meal would be anything but quiet.

Halfway through the meal, the dinner conversation shifted direction when Bob asked, "Did any of you read the article in *The Times* today about the 43-year-old pregnant woman?"

"What's so unusual about that?" Jim replied. "More and more women are having children later in life."

"It's not her age that's unusual," Bob said. "It's the reason she's having the baby. The article said she became pregnant in hopes that this child will become a bone marrow donor for her older daughter. Her 17-year-old has leukemia, and they can't find a matched donor anywhere. The odds that the new baby's marrow will match are pretty good. What do you think of her reason for having a child? Is it ethical? Is it a good reason for having a baby, especially in mid-life? What do the rest of you think?"

Bob studied the faces of the others seated at the table. The silence was heavy for several seconds as they considered an issue none of them had thought about before. Finally Mary broke the silence by saying, "I can't believe that anyone would bring a child into the world for that reason. That doesn't seem right to me."

"Oh, I don't know," Ted said. "I think their motivation is all right. I'm sure they'll love the child whether she becomes a donor or not."

Sue jumped in at this point. "I agree with Mary. That's not a good reason to have a child."

"It's not so bad," Ted continued. "Years ago couples who lived on farms had lots of children because they needed help with the plowing, planting and harvesting. What's the difference? What I'm interested in discussing is why *we* had children? Bob and Sue, why did you become parents? What about you, Frank and Mary? And what was our reason for having kids, Betsy? Did anyone ever bother to ask us?"

Ted paused to look from face to face. Each of his five friends had a different answer:

"We'd been married for six years and thought it was about time."

"Everyone else was having children, so we decided to."

"We thought it would help our marriage. Besides, you wouldn't believe the pressure we were getting from our parents."

"I just love children and couldn't wait."

"I felt—or we felt—that it was God's will and timing."

WE ALL HAD OUR REASONS

Ted proposed an interesting question and received five interesting answers. How would you answer his question? Why did you become a parent? What were your reasons for wanting to have children?

The authors of *The Parent Test* suggest four categories of motives for becoming a parent: ego, compensation, conformity and affection.

Ego

Some individuals and couples become parents for what they hope to get out of children and parenthood. Some examples of clearly egotistical reasons for wanting children include:

- to have a child who will look like me;
- to have a child who will carry on my admirable traits;
- to have a child who will be successful;
- to have someone who will carry on my name;
- to have someone to inherit family money or property;
- to have someone who will regard me as the greatest;
- to prove that I can do something well;
- to feel the pride of creation;
- to keep me young in heart;
- to help me feel fulfilled.

Compensation

Some adults feel that a child in the family will compensate them for a sense of lack in their lives or their marriage. Some compensatory motives for becoming a parent include:

- to make my marriage happier;
- to make up for my own unhappy family background;
- to make up for the lack of satisfaction in my job;
- to make up for my social isolation and lack of friends;
- to make me feel more secure about my masculinity or femininity;

Compensatory motives are very dangerous for parents and child alike. Many couples think that children will help solve their problems. Some couples want children in order to save their marriage. If a marriage needs saving, asking a baby to do the job is asking a person for skills he or she doesn't possess. A baby's presence may even distract the couple from analyzing and correcting their difficulties. Having a baby to save a bad marriage only makes the marriage worse! The same applies to having a baby in hopes of solving other problems.

Conformity
Some couples start families because they feel it is the thing to do. Conforming motives include:

- to be like most other people;
- to please my parents;
- to forestall social criticism.

Although not as dangerous as compensatory motives, conforming motives are also poor reasons for becoming a parent. The primary desire is not for the child, but to please someone else.

Affection

Some couples become parents because they are ready to pour their love and affection into a life they have created together. Affectionate motives for parenthood include:

- to have a real opportunity to make someone happy;
- to teach someone about all the beautiful things in life;
- to have the satisfaction of giving myself to someone else;
- to help someone grow and develop.

These are good reasons for wanting to become a parent.[1]

As you look over these four categories, what were your reasons for wanting to become a parent? Were your motives healthy or unhealthy?

No matter what your motives were for *becoming* a parent, the fact remains that you now *are* a parent. Whether your motives were good or bad in the past, you can't go back and change them. But you do have the opportunity to change how you function as a parent in the present and the future. Your focus must change from "Why didn't I have better motives?" to "How can I be a better, more nurturing, more communicative parent?"

All of us carry a mental image of a good parent and hold opinions about what qualities contribute to that image. We have an idea what parents should and shouldn't do and say. For most of us this image is highly idealistic. Parents are supposed to be all-knowing, all-caring and all-loving. That's not only idealistic, it's unrealistic!

Where did we get this lofty image? Our parents, our church and the media all contributed to our exaggerated expectations about parenting. Sometimes

> You look forward to parenting most of the time, but there are moments when you want to bail out, buy your child a one-way ticket to Siberia and become a non-parent again.

these idealistic, unrealistic expectations create a pressure which leads to frustration. As one mother said, "When I discovered that I couldn't meet my expectations, I didn't feel worthy to be a mother. I just felt like throwing in the towel. But then I realized that you can't send the kids back. You're stuck with them. And that's how I felt—stuck."

There is a big difference between something we are expected to do and something we desire to do. An expectation is a must, and when we can't fulfill it we become frustrated and depressed, and we feel "stuck." But a desire is something positive and pleasant we are shooting for. In order to keep ourselves from getting stuck in unrealistic expectations, let's talk about a general parenting goal and some secondary goals which will help us fulfill our desire to be good parents whose communication is positive and nurturing.

A Goal to Guide Us

Think with me for a moment about one specific area of your life: parenthood. How do you feel about yourself as a mother or a father? If you're like most parents, your feelings are mixed. You look forward to parenting most of the time, but there are moments when you want to bail out, buy your child a one-way ticket to Siberia and become a non-parent again. Parenting is demanding, and none of us is properly prepared. Your thoughts, attitudes and feelings about yourself as a parent will affect how you respond to your own child.

Imagine for a moment that you are sitting in my office. You are here with your spouse, or if you are a single parent, you are sitting by yourself. We've completed our introductions, and now I ask: "What are you endeavoring to accomplish with your children? What parenting goal would you like to reach by the time they leave your home? I would like you to give me your answer in 30 seconds."

Your response may be like that of a number of parents: "Thirty seconds isn't enough time to figure out the answer to a question like that." I wonder, however: Could it be that many of us have never given serious thought to the goals which could make a distinct difference in our parenting venture? If you have no overall goal, how will you determine your parenting style? What will guide you in developing a style of communication which will affirm and encourage your children? Without a goal you run the risk of watching your child default to a role like those described in chapter 1.

Let me suggest a general goal for parenting: *Our*

goal as parents is to empower our children to become mature and to release them to become independent from us and dependent on God. In addition to this general goal, you need to develop a blueprint of specific character goals for your children. We will discuss these secondary goals more fully in chapter 3.

Empowering Our Children to Maturity

Our job as parents is to empower our children to become mature. Maturity can imply many things. I would like to define it as the ability to contribute to the good of other people in a positive and constructive way. Perhaps this definition is best illustrated in 1 Thess. 5:11 where we are instructed to "encourage one another and build each other up." We want our children to grow up knowing how to love and serve people and assist them in their growth.

Most children don't develop these characteristics of maturity on their own. They must be empowered to maturity through the guidance of their parents. Jack and Judith Balswick describe the concept of empowering so well:

> Parents who are empowerers will help their children become competent and capable persons, who will in turn empower others. Empowering parents will be actively and intentionally engaged in various pursuits—teaching, guiding, caring, modeling—which will equip their children to become confident individuals able to relate to others. Parents who empower will help their children recognize the strengths and potentials within and find ways to enhance these qualities. Parental empowering is the affirmation of the child's abili-

ty to learn, grow, and become all that one is meant to be as part of God's image and creative plan.[2]

Parental love which is empowering enables rather than disables a child. When a parent holds on to a child too tightly, it's usually because he is trying to meet his own needs instead of the child's. Controlling, disabling parents jump in with "helping" comments like, "Here, let me do that for you. It's too hard for you." Some parents even speak for a child or finish his sentences for him. But these responses handicap the child, often causing him to feel, "Mom and Dad don't believe I'm capable of doing this for myself." Parental love affirms the child's adequacy and empowers him to maturity just as God's love affirms our adequacy in Christ and empowers us to maturity in Him.

How do we empower our children to achieve maturity? There are four techniques we must use: telling, teaching, participating and delegating. Each of these techniques relates to a different age level of the child and requires a different style of parental communication.

Telling. Young children need one-way communication up to age three to four while they are unable to do much on their own. They need clear direction and close supervision. This is not the style to use with older children or adolescents, because it keeps them dependent on you instead of encouraging independent thinking.

Teaching. This technique is used with children during their preschool and early elementary years. We instruct a child to do something he is capable of doing by using two-way, question-and-answer communication. Children at this age ask numerous questions and eventually can be encouraged to discover their own answers.

Participating. During the late elementary years parents take the role of player-coaches. Proper behavior is communicated more by example and interaction and less by direct instruction. Preteens are able to respond to this style of parenting. Parental control decreases as you encourage your children to learn to make decisions and carry out behavior on their own. A preteen needs to be encouraged to be an individual and should be given the freedom to learn through trial and error. But you are still there to provide needed support and consolation.

Delegating. Delegation is the final step toward empowering your child to maturity. It is used with mature preteens and adolescents who are able and willing to take responsibility and perform tasks on their own. When this occurs, you are empowering your child and he is also empowering you. You have now moved to the stage of reciprocal giving and receiving. Throughout the growth process you have given yourself to your child; now the child in his maturity begins to give to you. You have spent years communicating affirmation and encouragement to your child; now he verbally and nonverbally affirms and encourages you.

At this stage your child will probably make decisions differently than you do, and his conclusions will be different from yours. This is the evidence of maturity and independence.[3]

These four techniques must follow this order. If parents cannot adapt their techniques to meet the needs of the maturing child, growth will be hampered and the child will remain in his dependent state.

Releasing Our Children to Independence

The second phase of our general goal is to assist our children in moving from dependence on us, to semi-dependence, to independence from us and dependence on God, which is a true reflection of maturity. Time and time again I run into men and women in their 30s and 40s who are not yet independent of their parents. One woman lamented to me, "My parents are dead and gone, but they seem to reach out from the grave to control me—and I'm 39 years old! Why can't I be an independent adult?" The sad answer in most cases is that these parents did not release their children to independence. Our calling as parents is to enable our children to spread their wings and fly on their own.

One of the most dramatic images of a parent encouraging a child to become independent is the eagle. On numerous occasions my wife and I have watched these majestic birds soar in the Southern California mountains and in Wyoming's Grand Teton National Park. We have stood at the edge of the Snake River as eagles swooped gracefully down to the water, plunged their talons beneath the surface to capture a fish and then fly off to their nest with their catch.

But an eagle comes into the world looking anything but majestic and graceful. When an eaglet is hatched, it's just plain ugly! It's mostly neck with a tiny head and body attached. The eaglet's parents feed it often— to the point of gorging it—to assure its survival. It continues to eat and grow until it is as large as its parents. Finally it is ready for flying school, a major and necessary step to its independence and survival.

The mother eagle enters the nest and begins to coax and nudge the young eagle toward the edge. The eaglet digs its talons into the nest and resists with

---

God wants...children to become independent and free. He wants us to cooperate with Him in seeing our children released to independence.

---

all its strength. But the mother doesn't back down. She continues pushing until she finally shoves her young from the nest perched high on a rocky ledge! Can you imagine as a parent looking over the edge of a cliff and seeing your child falling? The young eagle is uncoordinated, but it is equipped for the fall. It finally spreads its wings and catches an updraft. It quickly learns how to flap its wings and soar. Soon it is hunting for its own food, and eventually it leaves the nest to establish its own home and family.

Like the eaglet, there comes a time when our children must be physically and emotionally set free from our control. God wants our children to become independent and free. He wants us to cooperate with Him in seeing our children released to independence. But sometimes it doesn't happen. Why not? We will discuss a number of reasons in chapter 4.

Several years ago when I was considering what it

meant to release my own child, I discovered a description of this process written by Christian psychiatrist Dr. John White. His words helped me understand my role. Perhaps they will assist you as well.

> In days gone by, market men in Covent Garden, London, used to sell caged nightingales. They captured the birds and blinded them by inserting hot needles into their eyes. Because nightingales sing in the dark, a liquid song bubbled almost endlessly from the caged and blinded birds. Man had enslaved and blinded them to gratify his delight in their music. More than this, he had enslaved them in such a manner that they could never again enjoy freedom. No one could set them free.
>
> To relinquish our children is to set them free. The earlier we relinquish them the better. If we unthinkingly view them as objects designed for our pleasure, we may destroy their capacity for freedom just as the Covent Garden men made nightingales "unfreeable." We may also cripple ourselves. Having made our children necessary to our happiness, we can so depend on them that we grow incapable of managing without them.
>
> Yet what is relinquishment? Clearly it must not mean avoiding our parental responsibilities. Our children need food, shelter, clothing, love and training, and it is our business to give them these. Nor does relinquishment mean to fail to teach our children respect and gratitude. Moreover, if we have the responsibility for their upbringing, we must have the authority to do whatever is necessary to fulfill that responsibility.

To understand what relinquishment is, we must first understand what God is like and what the essence of His relationship to us is. As He is to us, so must we (so far as possible) be to our children.

God's attitude as a parent...combines loving care and instruction with a refusal to force our obedience. He longs to bless us, yet he will not cram blessings down our throats. Our sins and rebellions cause him grief, and in his grief he will do much to draw us back to himself. Yet if we persist in our wrongdoing, he will let us find by the pain of bitter experience that it would have been better to obey him.

To relinquish your children does not mean to abandon them, however, but to give them back to God and in so doing to take your own hands off them. It means neither to neglect your responsibilities toward them nor to relinquish the authority you need to fulfill those responsibilities. It means to release those controls that arise from needless fears or from selfish ambitions.[4]

When parents do not release their children to independence and persist in being overprotective and restrictive, two opposite but negative responses may occur. Parents will either perpetuate the child's continued, unnatural dependence on them or provoke the child to make a drastic, radical break from parental control in order to establish his independence. Unfortunately the latter often results in a total break from all guidance and authority, including God's. The best releasing experience occurs when it is a positive process marked by the parents' blessing.

With the general goal of parenting and communication clearly in focus, it's time to consider parental roles and more specific, secondary goals.

FOR THOUGHT AND DISCUSSION

Share your responses with your spouse, a trusted friend or your study group.

1. Why did you become a parent? Rank the following motives from 1-4 in the order in which they influenced you to become a parent (rank your first motive with a 1, and so on). Have your spouse rank his or her motives. Then discuss your responses together and with your study group.

• Ego: I became a parent for what I could get out of it.
   My ranking _____
   My spouse's ranking _____

• Compensation: I became a parent to compensate for a lack in my life or marriage.
   My ranking _____
   My spouse's ranking _____

• Conformity: I became a parent because it was the thing to do.
   My ranking _____
   My spouse's ranking _____

• Affection: I became a parent because I was ready to pour my love into my child.
   My ranking _____
   My spouse's ranking _____

2. How would you rate your success at empowering

your children to maturity through telling, teaching, participating and delegating: excellent, good, fair or poor? How would your spouse rate his or her success? Why did you each respond as you did?

3. How would you rate your success at releasing your children to independence: excellent, good, fair or poor? How would your spouse rate his or her success? Why did you each respond as you did?

Notes
1. Williams Granzig and Ellen Peck, *The Parent Test* (New York: G.P. Putnams's and Sons, 1978), adapted from p. 19.
2. Jack O. Balswick and Judith K. Balswick, *The Family* (Grand Rapids, MI: Baker Book House, 1979), pp. 22,23. Used by permission.
3. Ibid., adapted from pp. 105-107.
4. Taken from *Parents in Pain* by John White. ©1979 by InterVarsity Christian Fellowship of the USA. Used by permission of InterVarsity Press, P.O. Box 1400, Downers Grove, IL 60515.

3

PARENTAL ROLES AND CHARACTER GOALS

Y OU can't talk about general or specific goals for raising and communicating with children without talking about parental roles. Let's consider three roles parents often assume in raising their children: the explorer, the farmer and the architect. Let's examine these roles and see if they help or hinder the general goal of empowering children to maturity and releasing them to independence.

THE EXPLORER-PARENT

Explorers are committed to discovering what is hidden or unknown. In the 1800s explorers ventured into unknown parts of our country to discover the character of the land and the best routes for travel. In so doing they faced many hazards. But in order for the land to be as useful and fruitful as possible, the explorers had to overcome the hazards and traverse the length and breadth of the land.

In a very real sense parents play the role of pioneering explorers. In order to properly teach, guide, encourage and nurture your child, you must patiently observe and study him to discover his unique personality traits and learning characteristics. The better you know your child, the better equipped you will be to prepare him for a meaningful life.

The key word for the communication of the explorer-parent is *ask*. Questions are the most direct way to explore your child's thoughts and feelings and to understand his hopes and dreams. To be successful, your questions should be general enough that they invite an honest response. If your children feel that you are prying into their lives, they will close up. Furthermore, your questions will be fruitless if you are judgmental about their responses or fail to keep in confidence everything they entrust to you as a secret.

Explorer-parents are in good position to implement the maturity and independence of their children. Their skill of asking questions is especially useful in the empowering techniques of teaching, participating and delegating. Furthermore, nonthreatening questions are an excellent tool for helping a child think about and identify his options for independence.

THE FARMER-PARENT

Parents are also like farmers. A farmer considers each plant unique. He doesn't force a potato to be an apple. Similarly, the farmer-parent recognizes the uniqueness of each child and nurtures that individual to full maturity and fruitfulness.

The farmer knows that his success at growing good crops is the result of a partnership:

> The idea of a partnership in farming is a strong one. We realize that not much will happen if the farmer doesn't throw himself wholeheartedly into bringing crops to fruition. That's his responsibility, and all his efforts lead to a productive harvest. But, it is equally true that nothing happens at all if God doesn't do His part. The farmer works with an absolute dependence on God to provide sun and rain. Even the farmer who does not believe in God knows, too well, the limitation of his powers.
>
> The active farmer wants pears to be pears, spinach to be spinach, avocados to be avocados and peas to be peas. He rejoices in the identity of what is planted and does everything to nurture each crop according to its own nature. While farmers are highly active in the nurturing of their crops, they must also learn to yield to circumstances over which they have no control. In the full knowledge of God's splendid grace, they must sometimes face the inexplicable.[1]

It is essential that you understand your partnership with God in parenting. You can't do it alone and expect a good crop.

The key word for the communication of the farmer-parent is *encourage*. A farmer who fails to encourage the growth of his plants through irrigation and cultivation will soon be out of business. And if you withhold words of love, affirmation and encouragement from your child, you will stunt his emotional and spiritual growth.

Farmer-parents are especially well-suited for empowering children to maturity and releasing them to independence. The communication style of encouragement builds confidence in the child to branch out on his own and try new endeavors, especially when the encouraging words are present after a disappointment or failure.

THE ARCHITECT-PARENT

Have you ever seen an architect at work? He goes to the drawing board and, in very intricate detail, designs the end product, whether it be a new home or a shopping mall. Many parents today are like architects. They believe they are totally responsible for what the child becomes. Architect parents mentally design all aspects of their child's life, including the end product. They have a very clear and definite picture of what they want their child to become. They carefully guide and control their child's activities, choices and relationships. They screen what he is exposed to and make sure he plays and socializes with the "right" children. The words "ought" and "should" are frequently heard in this family.

We all have a tendency to mold our children to match the design we have for their lives. If their unique tendencies threaten us, we try to make these differences disappear. Basically, we are comfortable with others who are like us. Thus we unwittingly attempt to fashion our children into a revised edition of ourselves. We want them to be created in our image. But that puts us in conflict with God who wants them to be created in His image.

It is very easy to abuse our parental authority by compelling our children to deny their individuality and conform to behaviors which violate their identity. As parents, one of our great challenges and delights is to honor our child's uniqueness and accept what cannot be changed in him. We are called to guide them,

---

If you withhold words of love, affirmation and encouragement from your child, you will stunt his emotional and spiritual growth.

---

not remake them. Appreciating their uniqueness can greatly reduce our frustration and our tendency to verbally abuse them.

Even when the child is grown up, the architect-parent's expectations are still operating. This may include selecting the child's vocation and the type of person he will marry. If the parents are successful in achieving their goals, they will probably end up with a highly dependent adult child who is riddled with guilt at every turn and spiritually indecisive and weak, with a distorted perspective of God. The attainment of such a goal can carry a high cost. These are the parents who often experience the big three: burnout, frustration and anger.

Unfortunately, the key word for the communication of the architect-parent is *dictate*. These parents often establish themselves as dictators in their children's lives. Parental communication is almost always a directive of some kind: where and where not to go, what and what not to do and say, etc.

Our role as a parent is not to supersede God's plan and design or interfere with His purpose. God is the one who has the ultimate goal and purpose for our children. In reality, He is the architect; we must yield to His design.[2]

> You must use a tailor-made blueprint for each child which contains a built-in flexibility for alterations along the way.

Even with all its potential dangers, the role of the architect-parent is not useless in contributing to a child's maturity and independence. The empowering technique of telling, which is vital to a child's first three or four years of growth, is often best served by this role. Problems arise, however, when the architect mentality dominates the parenting of older children who need more room to think and decide for themselves.

The parenting role I would like to suggest is a combination of all three. As we diligently explore the child and discover his unique qualities and gifts, we must cultivate and nurture his individuality without forcing him to become something he is not. A modified architectural approach can be implemented in the process as long as the plans are very flexible and custom-fitted to the child. When your communication is focused on nonthreatening, nonjudgmental questions and words of affirmation and encouragement, the directives you issue will more likely be heeded.

A BLUEPRINT FOR CHARACTER

In his excellent book, *Legacy of Love*, Tim Kimmel emphasizes the need to establish a blueprint for your child's character. His basic question is, "Do you have a plan for building your child's character?" Kimmel believes that in building your child's character you are leaving him a legacy of love. See his blueprint for character on the following pages.

In *Legacy of Love*, Tim Kimmel goes into great detail exploring and expanding on each of these character traits. It is the best treatment of character development I have ever seen. If you want further help in this area, I suggest you work through Kimmel's book.

You must use a tailor-made blueprint for each child which contains a built-in flexibility for alterations along the way. And you must always remember: The same free will which allowed Adam and Eve to make wrong choices still exists within every child. Regardless of how much you do, your children may elect not to go along with your blueprint.

Counterfeit Legacies

When you commit to a blueprint of character development with your children, your actions had better be consistent with your words. If you aren't personally committed to the skills, traits and goals you seek to develop in your children, you may end up passing on what Tim Kimmel calls counterfeit legacies: anger,

When my children move out from under my authority they need...

Decision-making skills:
In physical issues: exercise, nutrition, rest, etc.
In personal issues: finances, career, home life, etc.
In social issues: dating relationships, love, friendships, dealing with enemies, etc.

Character traits:
Faith, integrity, poise, discipline, endurance, and courage.

Commitment to life goals:
To love and obey God.
To love their spouse.
To love their children.
To be a good friend.
To work hard.
To invest their lives in others.

Ability to execute survival skills:
In the physical: manage a schedule, cook, swim, learn safety skills, drive, etc.
In the personal: live on a budget, manage a checkbook, know how to finish projects, keep belongings maintained, etc.
In the social: get along with others, confront, resolve, employ good manners, learn to stand alone if necessary, etc.
In the spiritual: share their faith, repent, be a friend of God, etc.

continued

Sustained relationships:
Ability to resolve conflict, serve others, communicate, listen, forgive, etc.

This list isn't the last word on the characteristics and skills we need to transfer to our children, but it can give you some ideas. By using the five areas in this checklist, we can develop an individual profile or blueprint for each one of our children and enhance it as he or she grows older.

These confidence builders have a "one-size-fits-all" character. Most of your responses to this checklist probably apply to all of your children. At the same time, these five statements allow us to consider the uniqueness of each child.

For instance, you may have a son that has a learning disability while his sister is a scholar. The kinds of skills you expect your son to master might be quite different from those you ask of your daughter. Gender should also be considered in the blueprint; the responsibilities of a young man on a date are different from those of a girl. Or you may have a child that excels in sports and will therefore wish to design his or her profile with that in mind.

The point is, leaving a legacy of love demands that we have a clear idea of what's required. Developing a blueprint for the finished product puts us miles ahead.[3]

fear, compromise, laziness, legalism, intimidation, labels, perfection and withdrawal. Contrast these negative characteristics with the legacy of genuine love.

Children reared in an angry environment suffer lives of emotional exhaustion. Punishment without relief is torture. Families who fail to deal with unresolved anger are sure to pass on their legacy to generation after generation—unless, of course, they receive a touch from the God of peace. . . .

Children left with a legacy of fear are hamstrung when they move into adulthood. And the fear they've lived around may someday become the fear they live by. . . .

Legalism is the by-product of life without grace. Many children reared in this type of environment bolt from it at first opportunity. Unfortunately, they often run from legalism to unbridled license. Their unbalanced childhood over-shifts and they spend their adulthood living life at the extremes.[4]

Guidelines for Change

You may be at a point right now where you would like to develop a blueprint for character development blueprint for your child, but some old habits stand in the way. Like many parents, maybe you have unwittingly fallen into a parenting style which you now understand to be less than ideal and perhaps even harmful to your child. You ask, "Where do I go from here? How do I change?" Change is possible, and here are some steps which will help you implement change in your parenting style:

Identify in writing what you want your parenting style to become and what you want to see

happen in your child. This step works best when father and mother are united in a team effort. After you have written your responses individually, share with each other your respective plans. Commit yourselves to help each other follow this new plan, hold each other accountable and pray for each other each day.

Communicate your new plan to your child. Sit down with your child and inform him about your goal for his life. Explain as much as he is capable of comprehending about how he can expect you to respond to him under this new approach. Some parents have called this a "realignment session" because it gives new direction for family life.

It's important that during this session you assure your child of your love for him and that you are committed to the best for his life. One parent phrased it this way: "I love you, and I cherish our relationship. I'm glad you are my daughter. But I also want you to know that it is very important to me to be a good parent. You deserve the best."

If you are working to change a bad parenting pattern such as being overly strict or legalistic, describe your old pattern in terms simple enough for your child to understand. You may say, "There have been times when I was overly strict with you and have not listened to what you wanted or needed. Sometimes I have been more concerned with what I thought was proper instead of what was best for your growth."

It is also important that you let your child know how you felt about how you acted in the past. Reassure your child that he was not responsible for the way you treated him. You may say, "The way I treated you was not the way I wanted to treat you. It's hard for me to admit it, but I know I probably made life hard for you the way I acted." If you need to apologize to your child or ask forgiveness for specific actions or words, now is the time to do so.

Also during the realignment session, ask your child to share with you how he felt under your old parenting style. Then ask how he might feel under the new approach you have described. Don't press your child for an immediate response; he may need time to think about it. Then ask your child to pray for you in your new endeavor.

Implement your new plan. To help you get started, read your new written plan aloud every morning and afternoon for 30 days. During that month, evaluate your progress at the end of each week—first by yourself, then with your spouse or a trusted friend. Don't expect instant change in yourself or your child. We all change gradually, but steady growth tends to be more permanent.

FOR THOUGHT AND DISCUSSION

Share your responses with your spouse, a trusted friend or your study group.

1. Complete the following statements as they apply to you:

• My greatest strength as an explorer-parent is . . .

• My greatest weakness as an explorer-parent is . . .

• My greatest strength as a farmer-parent is . . .

• My greatest weakness as a farmer-parent is . . .

• My greatest strength as an architect-parent is . . .

• My greatest weakness as an architect-parent is . . .

2. Based on Tim Kimmel's blueprint for character, list one or two primary goals you would like to set for your children in each of the following categories:

• Decision-making skills:

• Character traits:

• Life goals:

• Survival skills:

• Relationships:

Notes
1. Used with permission by David C. Cook Publishing Co. *Discovering Your Child's Design* by Ralph Mattson and Thom Black © 1989, available at your local Christian bookstore.
2. Ibid., adapted from pp. 189-191.
3. From the book *Legacy of Love* by Tim Kimmel, copyright 1989 by Tim Kimmel. Published by Multnomah Press, Portland, Oregon 97266. Used by permission.
4. Ibid., pp. 223,224,227.

4

ARE YOU PARENTING WITH- OUT A COMPASS?

SEVERAL years ago I owned my own boat. I'm not talking about a large yacht or anything close to it. My boat was a 16-footer with a small outboard motor. I used it for fishing the lakes and ocean in southern California.

Just after I purchased my boat, but before I had all the equipment I needed to use it safely, a friend and I put in at the Long Beach harbor intending to motor out to the breakwater. It was bright and clear in the harbor until we came out of the channel, and then we hit dense, wet fog. I couldn't see more than 20 feet ahead of me. But I had been in this large expanse of water inside the breakwater before, and I felt that if I traveled slowly I could find my way to the bait barge. So we kept going in what I thought was the right direction, confident that the bait barge would appear before us in the soup any minute.

Suddenly I saw something in front of us. But as we got closer, I realized that it wasn't the breakwater; it was a large island covered with oil wells. I couldn't figure out how we got there, but when we asked one of the oil workers for directions to the breakwater, I discovered that we had veered off course a few degrees early in our trip. For the first 100 yards or so, those few degrees didn't make too much difference. But the farther we traveled, the wider the gap became between where we wanted to go and where we were actually headed. Since I didn't have a compass, I was off course and didn't even know it. Needless to say, after that outing I bought a compass for the boat!

DRIFTING TOWARD DYSFUNCTIONAL TRAITS

What about you: Do you have a compass to guide you as a parent? How would you know if you drifted off course in your parenting roles, goals and communication? In these next two chapters I want to share with you a number of parenting "compass points" which will help you determine if you are on course in some critical areas of your style of parenting and communicating with your children.

As you examine the characteristics of a dysfunctional home in this chapter and the myths of parenting in chapter 5, don't be discouraged if you discover that you are off course a few degrees in your parenting. Nobody's perfect. You may be reflecting some dysfunctional traits you inherited from the home in which you were raised. You may be off course because you have been sailing without a compass;

you didn't know any better. But the sooner you recognize that you are not headed in the direction you want to go, the easier it will be to get back on course.

The first step in correcting your parenting course is to identify some elements of family atmosphere that you *don't* want in your home. There are nine of them in the following pages for you to consider. From here you can take the necessary steps to move back on course. Subsequent chapters in this book will help you with these course corrections. For additional help on this subject, you may want to read *Adult Children: The Secrets of Dysfunctional Families* (Health Communications, Inc.), by John and Linda Friel, and *Always Daddy's Girl* (Regal Books), by this author.

Verbal/Emotional Abuse

Abuse is the most devastating element of a dysfunctional home. When you hear about abuse, perhaps you immediately think of physical or sexual abuse. Tragically, these forms of abuse occur all too frequently—even in Christian homes. But verbal and emotional abuse is even more frequent in our homes. Obvious forms of verbal/emotional abuse include parents screaming at their children or making disparaging remarks to them. Yet subtler forms of abuse are just as painful and damaging. Here are several examples:

- Ignoring a child by not listening, not responding, etc.
- Giving a child choices which are only negative, such as saying, "Either you eat every bite of your dinner or you will get a spanking."
- Constantly projecting blame onto a child.
- Distorting a child's sense of reality, such as saying,

"Your brother doesn't do drugs. He's just having a hard time. You're imagining things."
- Overprotecting a child.
- Blaming others for a child's problems.
- Communicating confusing double messages to the child, such as saying, "Yes, I love you. Now, for crying out loud, don't bother me. Can't you see I'm busy!"

Perfectionism

Perfection in parenting is not often considered an unhealthy symptom. But it is a common source of many family problems. A perfectionist is often angry because he cannot live up to his own standards. As a parent, this person is also angry at his children because they can't live up to his standards either, reminding him of his own inadequacies.

Perfectionists usually communicate their unrealistic demands to their children through many means: verbal rebukes and corrections, disapproving scowls, critical harping, etc. The words "should" and "ought" seem to dominate the communication of a perfectionistic parent.

Sometimes perfectionistic messages are hidden or implied in what sounds like a message of affirmation. For example:

- "You've always been an obedient child. You've never given me a minute of trouble." Translation: "Don't change or rock the boat. Always conform to what I want, and I'll be happy."
- "You've always been able to adjust and to be positive." Translation: "Always be pleasant, adaptable

and easy-going. Don't get upset. Bury your unpleasant feelings."

- "I expect the best from you. You're the one child I can depend upon." Translation: "You are the one person who can make my life fulfilling. Sacrifice yourself for me. Never, never disappoint me."

This kind of communication is a form of verbal torture. Children end up feeling substandard: "Why bother trying to be good?" they rationalize. "I'll never measure up anyway."

Unbending rules, a super-strict family life-style and a legalistic belief system make for an overly rigid, negative family experience.

Rigidity

Unbending rules, a super-strict family life-style and a legalistic belief system make for an overly rigid, negative family experience. Life is governed by routine. Relationships and events are strictly controlled. The joy and surprise of spontaneity in the family is smothered by responsibility and duty.

Rigidity is seen in parent-child communication in statements like: "We don't ever do that"; "This is the only way for this to be done"; "Don't ever do anything to embarrass our family"; "We always follow our family tradition for our activities on Sunday"; "No, we cannot change our schedule. You will just have to skip that activity."

Silence

Some parents would give a lot to bring a little silence into their noisy homes. That's normal. But some parents in dysfunctional homes insist on a gag rule for the family. "We don't talk outside the walls of this home. We don't share family secrets or ask others for help if we're having a problem." Everything is to be kept within the family. No one else is supposed to know about their conflicts or problems.

Children sworn to forced silence grow up believing that they have to handle the burdens of life by themselves. They don't allow themselves to share their struggles with others, even those who may be able to help them.

Repression

Identifying and expressing emotions in a positive way is healthy. Over-controlling and repressing them is asking for future difficulty. I talk with many husbands and wives who grew up in homes where emotions were denied and repressed. Then they carried this unhealthy trait into their marriages, and it became the death sentence for the relationship. God created us as emotional beings, and our feelings cannot be bottled up, especially negative feelings like anger, fear, depression, etc. These emotions must be expressed creatively and positively within the context of a loving, accepting family. When we repress emotions we are denying reality. Children of emotionally repressed parents learn to wear happy masks all the time, masks which only serve to perpetuate their pain.

Clogging the emotional pipelines by repressing or denying feelings leads to many physical problems. Repression can even trigger numerous compulsive behaviors such as eating disorders. We think that if we repress our feelings they will go away. But they don't; they're simply dammed up. Eventually the dam will crack and burst, and the emotions will explode unchecked, usually in a hurtful way to all involved.

Some families are just too serious. They don't know how to loosen up, let go, play and have fun.

Triangulation

This term describes a communication trait in many dysfunctional families. In triangulation, the parents use the child as a go-between. For example, Father tells six-year-old Tommy, "Go see if your mother is still upset with me. Take her this flower, and tell her I love her." So little Tommy sets out on his errand of reconciliation for his father, and feels quite proud of his assignment.

But Mother says to Tommy, "Tell your father I don't want his flower. Tell him it will take more than a flower to make up with me this time." In his mind, little Tommy has failed in his mission and must convey the bad tidings to his father, who may in turn take his anger or disappointment out on Tommy.

In triangulation, the child is caught in the middle of adult issues he can't handle. He is being used in an unhealthy way. This too is a form of abuse. If triangulation is a regular pattern in the family, the child may become a guilt collector, feeling responsible for everything that goes wrong in the family.

Lack of Fun

Some families are just too serious. They don't know how to loosen up, let go, play and have fun. They live by work ethic mottoes such as "Be serious," "Work hard or somebody will get ahead of you" and "Play is a waste of time." Their communication lacks the playful teasing, story- and joke-telling and lighthearted banter which every family needs. And on the rare occasions when these families *do* try to have fun, they often end up hurting each other because they don't know how to play.

Recently I talked to two different men who told me essentially the same story: "I grew up in a family that didn't have fun. I feel like I missed my childhood. I feel robbed. I never got to be a child." How sad.

Martyrdom

We don't hear too much about martyrs today, yet many exist in dysfunctional families. Martyrdom in this sense is not a calling from the Lord or a spiritual gift. It's a distorted sense of self-denial. Martyr families have a high tolerance for personal abuse and pain. Martyr parents tell their children that others always come first, no matter what the cost. Many of these children grew up watching their parents punish themselves through overwork, eating disorders, substance abuse, etc.

Children of martyr parents often grow up seeing themselves as victims, pleasers or martyrs. Self-denial is the name of the game, but it's destructive because it's self-deprecating.

Entanglement

Have you ever reached into a drawer or closet for extension cords and found them tangled together? Probably. Were you able to use them to their fullest extent in that condition? Probably not. Entanglement happens in families as well. The mother, father and children become emotionally entangled in each other's lives to the point that their individual identities are blurred and diminished. Each family member pokes his nose into the others' business. Mom makes the problems of Dad and the kids her own. Dad and the kids do the same. If one family member is depressed, so is everyone else. And they're so emotionally entangled that each person blames the others for his condition.

It's as though the whole family is sitting together on a giant swing. When one member goes up, the others go up with him. When one goes down, so do the others. Individual members don't think or feel for themselves. In time they begin to wonder, "Who am I?" Their individual identities are lost in their entangled relationship.[1]

Entanglement also impedes parent-child communication. It's difficult for a child to carry on a conversation in an entangled family because someone is always chiming in with his opinion. Sometimes discussions are never completed because everybody keeps jumping in and out of the conversation. And you can't count on anyone keeping a confidence. Anything shared with one family member will eventually be shared with all others.

Use the "For Thought and Discussion" exercise below to help you evaluate the presence of these traits in your family of origin and your present family. If you find that these tendencies existed in your family of origin, now is the time to take action. You cannot change the past, but you can begin to change your present response to past events. I encourage you to read the two books mentioned earlier. They will help you deal with the dysfunctional tendencies in your past and their present influence on you.

If the exercise below reveals that these traits are significantly present in your current family, you can make course corrections in your present family life as well. Discuss this chapter together as a couple, considering the positive direction you want to take. If you are a single parent, discuss these issues with a trusted friend. Healthy family relationships and a positive home atmosphere and communication style can be achieved!

FOR THOUGHT AND DISCUSSION

Share your responses with your spouse, a trusted friend or your study group.

1. On a scale of 0 (meaning "never present") to 10 (meaning "always present"), rate the presence of these 9 dysfunctional traits in both your family of origin and present family.

- Verbal/Emotional Abuse
    Family of origin   0 1 2 3 4 5 6 7 8 9 10
    Present family   0 1 2 3 4 5 6 7 8 9 10

- Perfectionism
  Family of origin 0 1 2 3 4 5 6 7 8 9 10
  Present family   0 1 2 3 4 5 6 7 8 9 10

- Rigidity
  Family of origin 0 1 2 3 4 5 6 7 8 9 10
  Present family   0 1 2 3 4 5 6 7 8 9 10

- Silence
  Family of origin 0 1 2 3 4 5 6 7 8 9 10
  Present family   0 1 2 3 4 5 6 7 8 9 10

- Repression
  Family of origin 0 1 2 3 4 5 6 7 8 9 10
  Present family   0 1 2 3 4 5 6 7 8 9 10

- Triangulation
  Family of origin 0 1 2 3 4 5 6 7 8 9 10
  Present family   0 1 2 3 4 5 6 7 8 9 10

- Lack of Fun
  Family of origin 0 1 2 3 4 5 6 7 8 9 10
  Present family   0 1 2 3 4 5 6 7 8 9 10

- Martyrdom
  Family of origin 0 1 2 3 4 5 6 7 8 9 10
  Present family   0 1 2 3 4 5 6 7 8 9 10

- Entanglement
  Family of origin 0 1 2 3 4 5 6 7 8 9 10
  Present family   0 1 2 3 4 5 6 7 8 9 10

2. For each trait you rated 4 or higher for your present family, state the positive characteristic which needs to replace it. How will you work toward implementing these characteristics in the coming week?

Note

1. H. Norman Wright, *Always Daddy's Girl* (Ventura, CA: Regal Books, 1989), adapted from pp. 140-155.

5

THE MYTHS OF PARENTING

IF you have been a parent for any length of time, no doubt some of your original theories about parenting have changed over the years. Mine certainly have. Most of us changed our thinking because we discovered that what we originally believed about parenting was untrue. What first seemed to be fact turned out to be a myth.

There are several myths about parenting we must continually avoid when plotting our course as nurturing, communicative parents. Like myths of other kinds, the myths of parenting are widely accepted as truth. But they're not true. And even though we have to live *with* them, we don't have to live *by* them. Sadly, parents who live by these myths about parenting often experience disillusionment and discouragement. They are tied in knots because it's impossible to live up to these ideals. If we don't change some of our false beliefs about parenting, we will stagnate and lock ourselves and our families into untruth.

Let's consider three popular myths of parenting. There are others in circulation, and perhaps you could add a few from your own experience. But if you change your beliefs in these three areas, you will be well on your way toward successful parenting and communication.

MYTH 1: TOTAL PARENTAL INVOLVEMENT

The first myth of parenting claims that good parents involve themselves totally in their children every day. I hope you are enthused about being a parent. You need enthusiasm in order to do a good job, but you don't need overenthusiasm. You need to be involved with your children, but you don't need total involvement to the point that they are the center of your attention every moment of the day.

Parental overinvolvement can be seen in parent-child communication. Overinvolved parents make statements such as, "I hope you appreciate all that I do for you" or "How dare you not want to go? Don't you realize what I've given up for you to be involved in this activity?" Overinvolvement can lead to excessive expectations and demands on a child because of all the sacrifices the parent makes. A parent's communication may reflect self-pity, martyrdom or guilt in order to control the child, such as, "Can't you see everything I am doing for you?" or "I am glad to give up my class in order to be with you, even though I will miss some important information."

Some of the most frustrated parents I've met were overenthused and overinvolved. They dropped out of all activities not related to parenting in order to give their children their total time and attention. They refused to allow anyone else to influence or care for their children in any way. Some parents of three-year-olds have told me that they have never left their children with baby-sitters. They want their children with them at all times. That's unnecessary and unhealthy overinvolvement.

Overattentive parents give and give to their children without teaching them to take responsibility for themselves and their needs when they are old enough. These parents take on many projects and activities which benefit their children but bring imbalance to their lives as adults.

Parents who fall victim to this myth often have too much of their self-worth tied into the responses of their children. This leads to overly rigid standards for both the parent and child. They spend every possible minute of time with the child, allowing no real free time or space for either. They even feel guilty taking an evening for themselves or going away for the weekend with their spouse. In short, this parent feels completely indispensable to his or her children.

When you begin to feel indispensable to your children, you will end up in a vicious circle of fatigue and guilt. You get so tired from your involvement that you allow others to pitch in and help you. But then you feel guilty for not doing your parental duty, which pushes you into greater involvement and increased fatigue.

Recently I talked with several sets of parents who felt exhausted and trapped. As one couple put it, "We've always tried to be available for our children, and we've encouraged them to participate in activities that interested them. But we haven't had a Saturday to do what we wanted to do for months. John has soccer at 10:00 A.M., Kenny at 11:30 and Kelly at 2:00. The teams always go somewhere to eat afterwards, so guess who the chauffeur is! Then there's football in the fall and Little League in the spring and summer. We're so tired of just giving and giving."

Overinvolvement also leads to disappointment and frustration, and eventually to parental burnout. You have nothing more to give because you haven't taken time to replenish yourself. Even with sufficient sleep you rarely feel rested. You drag yourself from one event to another. You wonder, "Where is the joy of parenting that people talk about?" The conditions are now right for anger and resentment.

Jim and Helen were the angry victims of parental overinvolvement. "I'm the outward screamer," Helen said. "I don't hit the kids physically, but I sure let them have it emotionally. Jim screams too, but he screams silently inside. I wish he'd vent his anger and frustration to someone. My outbursts aren't good for the kids, but his aren't good for him. But we don't know what to do about it."

Tell-tale Signs

How do you know if you are an overly involved parent? What's the difference between being an attentive and loving parent and an overly involved parent? Here are some signs of possible parental overinvolvement:

- You insist that your child eat everything on his plate.
- You restrict your child from some activities because you're afraid he will get hurt.

- You act as your school-aged child's personal valet—dressing him, tying his shoes and doing other things for him that he is capable of doing for himself.
- You constantly remind your child or teen to wear warm clothes on a cold day.
- You regularly do homework for the child.
- You give the child no household responsibilities.
- You walk an older child to school each day.
- You don't allow others to care for or baby-sit the child.
- You only allow your teens to go out with the friends you select for him.
- You always pick up after the child, including his room.

Some of these responses are found only in the parents of small children, but many are found in parents of school-aged and teenaged children as well. And there are many overly attentive parents who make decisions for their children into adulthood. Such overinvolvement does not prepare the child to become a responsible, independent adult. Constant parental overattentiveness smothers a child's natural quest for independence.[1]

Escaping Overinvolvement

Let me tell you about another couple who took a different approach to parenting. They thoroughly discussed their goals for their children as well as their individual and marital goals. All their goals were considered in their allocation of their time and energy.

Their children all wanted to be involved in sports, so the family sat down at the beginning of the season and discussed the cost in terms of time and energy. Each child was allowed to choose two sports a year to participate in, with the understanding that Mom and Dad could not attend every game. On the weekends that Mom and Dad were out of town, each child was responsible to obtain a ride to and from the game with a friend. Special games which Mom and Dad could not attend were videotaped by a friend. Later the entire family had a great time watching the videos together.

Constant parental overattentiveness smothers a child's natural quest for independence.

What are your expectations for being involved with your children? Are they realistic? Are you attempting to be supermom or superdad? For this family, careful planning allowed the children to be involved in many activities without the parents becoming overinvolved.

Our task as parents is to teach our children responsibility and literally let go of them at different stages of their development. Perhaps we need to make a public announcement occasionally to remind ourselves of each new stage, something like: "Our child is no longer in kindergarten; he is now in elementary school. His new freedoms will be..."; "Our child has turned 13. We will treat her as an adolescent and encourage her growth. We believe that she will begin to respond as a young woman."

What would happen if you sat down with your

child on his birthday and discussed with him what he thinks his next year will be like. Ask about his expectations for himself, as well as for you as his parents. Ask him how you can best help him during the coming year. Share with him some of your hopes and expectations for him. Some parents summarize these discussions in writing for reference through the year. Such conferences reduce the frustration and verbal abuse for both parents and children.

Years ago when our daughter Sheryl was approaching the significant milestone of her 16th birthday, we decided that it was important to clarify everyone's expectations and guidelines for two major activities on the horizon of her life: dating and driving. Joyce, Sheryl and I each thought about what we wanted to include in these guidelines. Then we sat down together and discussed our thoughts. There was much give and take. Finally we agreed on a covenant and set of guidelines which would remain in effect until Sheryl turned 18. At that point she would be on her own. Sheryl's guidelines for dating and driving included:

1. Before using the car I will ask Mom or Dad for permission and explain my purpose for using it.
2. Before I go somewhere my homework and piano practice will be thoroughly completed.
3. During the school year I will be allowed to drive to church on Wednesday nights, but I cannot drive anyone home afterward without prior permission.
4. I will not allow anyone else to use the car under any circumstances.
5. I will be allowed to drive up to 35 miles a week

at no charge, after which I must pay for any additional mileage.

6. I will not give rides to hitchhikers under any conditions, nor will I accept a ride from a stranger if I have difficulty with the car.

7. I will either wash the car or have it washed once every three weeks.

8. In case I am the cause of an accident, I will pay half of the deductible charge and half of the increase in the insurance premiums.

Discovering the proper balance of parental involvement is a constant struggle. But we must continue to look for the center point between too much and too little structure and order for the children, between too much and too little scheduling and between family togetherness and individual privacy. Our rules must be consistent, not contradictory. Family flexibility must win out over rigidity.

MYTH 2: TOTAL PARENT RESPONSIBILITY

The second major myth of parenting states that the child's success or failure depends entirely on the parents. Many Christian parents struggle with this myth, believing that they are responsible when their children make decisions contrary to the way they were raised. You can hear it in their conversations: "Where did we go wrong?"; "How could this have happened to us?"; "Where was God in all this?"; "If only we had raised them better"; "How could he turn away from us after all the guidance we gave him?"

These parents quote the promise in Prov. 22:6 as proof of their assumed responsibility: "Train a child in the way he should go, and when he is old he will not turn from it" (NIV). They treat this passage as a divine guarantee. So if the child turns from "the way he should go," the parents naturally assume that they have failed to train him adequately.

But is this verse an absolute promise or a general principle? Psychiatrist John White feels that the Proverbs were written as probabilities of likely occurrences instead of ironclad promises. Solomon's purpose was to share his God-directed observations on the way human nature and God's creation operate. But some of his observations have been lifted out of context. Prov. 22:6 has been made to stand by itself as a promise from God. Those who claim this verse as a guarantee believe that a child can be programmed so thoroughly that his course is determined. If the child fails, they assert, the parents failed.

But if we follow that logic we would have to accuse God of failing as a father. Think about Adam and Eve. Did God make any mistakes in fathering them? Absolutely not! Didn't He respond to them with wisdom, love and care and surround them with a perfect environment? Yes, positively! Yet in spite of God's perfect parenting, Adam and Eve chose to depart from the way God wanted them to go.

God has given us the same freedom He gave Adam and Eve: the freedom to choose between good and evil. Your children have that same freedom. You are responsible to love them, care for them and surround them with a positive, nurturing environment. But you are not responsible for the direction they choose in life. Total parental responsibility is a myth, and the guilt, frustration and self-condemnation which results from it is totally unfounded.[2]

MYTH 3: TOTAL PARENT ENJOYMENT

The third widely accepted myth is that parenting is a totally rewarding job, and that you will always enjoy your children. This idea is only partially true at best. Yes, parenting can be rewarding and enjoyable a good deal of the time. But not always. There will be times of frustration and anger which will make you ask, "Where do I go to resign from being a parent?" There will be times of disappointment and heartache which prompt you to wonder, "Why didn't we remain childless?"

Over the years I have heard many parents comment about their unrealistic expectations for total enjoyment of their children. Unfortunately, many parents communicate their disappointment to their children through comments like: "I never dreamed raising you would be such a chore"; "After we realized what it takes to take care of you, we decided not to have any more children"; "I can't wait for you and your brother to go to camp so I can have some rest"; "I'm looking forward to the day you're in school so I can get out of the house and go back to work."

Whether you utter these comments in an outburst of frustration or in jest, it could take your children years to recover from them.

Why is parenting less that totally enjoyable? There are several reasons:

- When the results we expect from parenting aren't always the results we get, our identity and self-worth are threatened. A husband and wife may be successful in their marriage, their jobs and other endeavors. But if their child doesn't live up to their expectations—and no child will completely—the parents may feel like failures.

- A child places many time demands on his parents. Mom and Dad soon learn that their time is not their own any more. Most parents don't usually enjoy a child's intrusion on their schedule.

- Much of parenthood requires skills which are learned by doing. Many parents experience guilt and anxiety from the often-repeated dilemma of not knowing what to do for the child.

- Children suffer frequent lapses in physical and emotional control, so their parents must exhibit tremendous self-control in parenting situations which provoke them to anger.

- Communicating with children is different from communicating with adults. Adults enjoy free and open communication, but parent-child communication is limited to the understanding of the child. Adults give, receive and carry out instructions easily. A parent must often repeatedly remind and correct a child before instructions are finally carried out.

- Parenthood is restrictive on activities, especially for the mother. Picture yourself in the bind of many formerly employed mothers. You have enjoyed a measure of independence and accomplishment in your job. But now you have exchanged your job for motherhood, plunging you into the insecurity and indecisiveness of a task where your skills are untested. Your feelings of competence and your ability to get things done begin to diminish. A husband's support and involvement can definitely be a stabilizing force during this time.

- Parenthood changes a mother's view of self and others. Having a child tends to prompt a woman toward greater selflessness and concern for the care of another than she had before. She must rely more on her husband than before. As she takes care of her baby, she needs to be taken care of herself, whether she wants to be or not.

The parenting pressures on a mother are evident in many ways. Roger Gould, M.D., describes some of these pressures in his book *Transformations*:

In her daily experience with a child, a mother's time is not her own. She has to respond constantly to unclear verbal and preverbal demands from her child. Often she has no idea what to do; many times no good solution is available, so she'll suffer guilt and anxiety no matter what she does. The child constantly explores the boundaries of her patience and power. When the child's control lapses, her own control is required. She must consider using force on a helpless human being who sometimes invades her bodily privacy and psychological integrity like a monstrous, consuming enemy. She deals with the world of child rearing, where hundreds of experts give contradictory advice; the outcome can't be measured for fifteen to twenty years. She has to process this advice through her intuition and a constant stream of her own childhood memories dredged up by her child's dilemmas. And she must do all this with others—mother, mother-in-law, neighbors and school teachers—looking over her shoulder, marking her report card, measuring her against their own standards. Though it would be a relief to give up and follow some set of packaged rules, she must dare to be different—the fate of her child depends on her decisions. Besides, no set of rules seems exactly right.[3]

ARE YOU LIVING A MYTH?

Are you constantly fatigued and plagued by feelings of resentment, guilt, frustration and anger as a parent? Do you question your identity and self-worth? Check your parental beliefs and expectations. You may be

> As a parent do you question your identity and self-worth? Check your parental beliefs and expectations. You may be the victim of parenting myths.

the victim of parenting myths. Perhaps you can relate to the three we have discussed. Now is the time to reassess your parenting beliefs. If you don't, you may continue in parental burnout and begin to dislike your children. You may even end up feeling that your children are out to get you! Even worse, you may begin to say to yourself, "I just don't care anymore."

Have you ever felt this way? It may have happened to you in the past. If so, what did you do about it? It may be happening to you now. It could happen to you in the future. The good news is that it can be overcome and prevented!

What are your beliefs about parenting? Have you stated them in writing? What you believe about parenting will determine your communication style with your children and help you avoid the communication problems we will discuss in the following chapters.

FOR THOUGHT AND DISCUSSION

Share your responses with your spouse, a trusted friend or your study group.

1. To what extent has your parenting been influenced by the myths of parenting discussed in this chapter? Mark an *x* on each line below showing the extent of each myth's influence in you. Mark an *s* on each line showing the extent of each myth's influence on your spouse.

• Myth 1: Good parents involve themselves totally in their children every day.

No   Total
Influence .... Influence

• Myth 2: The child's success or failure depends entirely on the parents.

No   Total
Influence .... Influence

• Myth 3: Parenting is a totally rewarding job; you will always enjoy your children.

No   Total
Influence .... Influence

2. Write down several of your beliefs about parenting. You may want to begin by rephrasing the three myths above to reflect what you now believe about parental involvement, responsibility and reward.

• Parenting is . . .

• Parenting is . . .

• Parenting is . . .

• Parenting is . . .

• Parenting is . . .

Notes

1. From *Mother Love, Mother Hate,* Anne Grizzle © 1988 by Anne Grizzell & William Proctor. Reprinted by permission of Ballantine, A Division of Random House, Inc.

2. James C. Dobson, *Parenting Isn't for Cowards* (Dallas, Texas: WORD Incorporated, 1987), adapted from pp. 184,186.

3. *Transformations.* Copyright © 1978 by Roger Gould, M.D. Reprinted by permission of SIMON & SCHUSTER, INC.

Part II

POLLUTION-FREE COMMUNICATION

6

LET'S BAN THE TOXIC VERBAL WEAPONS

laska, 1988. Prince William Sound. The *Exxon Valdez*. These words remind us of one of our country's worst environmental disasters. The giant oil tanker spilled 11 million gallons of crude oil into the Sound contaminating more than 1,200 miles of shoreline. The spill was responsible for the deaths of 1,000 sea otters and more than 100,000 birds, including 150 bald eagles. Losses to the fishing industry exceeded $100 billion. The aftermath of the oil spill will be with us for years.

Contamination has occurred in our cities as well. Toxic materials thoughtlessly dumped into landfills years ago are coming back to haunt us. Toxic fumes are now seeping into homes constructed over these landfills, and entire communities have been evacuated because of the danger of toxicity.

On an international scale, the super powers continue to argue about the stockpile of nuclear weapons posing imminent danger to the entire world. Some weapons are being dismantled and destroyed while others are being unilaterally reduced in number.

Just as our world has problems with dangerous contamination, toxicity and weapons, so do our homes—even our Christian homes. We often poison and wound each other, especially our children, with the words we use. You may have grown up with parents who used words as weapons, and you hoped you wouldn't do the same with your children. But you will probably repeat the pattern in some way—unless you become the transition person to break the pattern and develop healthy patterns of communication which reflect the presence of Jesus Christ. Such a change is possible!

VERBAL WEAPONS MUST BE DISMANTLED

I call them toxic weapons—those cruel, caustic, bitter, degrading and judgmental words we use to hurt our children. They both contaminate and wound, poison and destroy our children emotionally. Our words are often launched as verbal missiles to attack a child's behavior, appearance, intelligence, competence or value as a person.

James recognized the potentially toxic nature of the words we speak:

> The human tongue can be tamed by no man. It is (an undisciplined, irreconcilable) restless evil, full of death-bringing poison. With it we bless the Lord and Father, and with it we curse men who

were made in God's likeness! Out of the same mouth come forth blessing and cursing. These things, my brethren, ought not to be so (3:8-10).

Words bruise and batter on the inside like physical blows bruise and lacerate the skin. That's why we call it verbal abuse. We're often unaware of the damage our words cause because we can't see the inner cuts and bruises. Even when the verbal assault stops, the emotional damage continues within the child into adulthood. Think back to your childhood: Were toxic verbal weapons used in your home? Do you still carry the inner scars from poisoned, hurtful words launched at you by your parents, brothers, sisters or friends?

Direct Verbal Abuse

Verbal abuse can be direct, open and obvious. For example, I've heard parents in public call their children stupid, retarded or worthless. I've heard hurtful parental put-downs like, "You'll never amount to anything" and "Can't you do anything right?" The following list of statements are also forms of direct verbal abuse:

- "You could be going with them if you hadn't blown it." This parent is abusing his child by reminding him of his misbehavior.
- "Isn't grounding fun? You seem to be having such a good time! We ought to do this more often!" Taking delight in your child's suffering is abusive.
- "With every dish you wash, just remember what a disgusting little creep you've been." This verbal attack hurtfully projects failure onto the child.
- "Sure, you can use the car. Your brother's wings

are clipped, and he won't be needing it." It's abusive to take a cheap verbal shot at a child either behind his back or in front of his face.

- "I can't find my watch! Did you steal that, too?" That's verbally kicking a child when he is down, and it hurts.
- "Get in there and cook supper! You need the practice. At the rate you're going, you'll have your own family to cook for by the time you graduate from high school. Graduate? Did I say graduate? Ha! That's a laugh!" Comments like these are forms of verbal harassment.
- "Yes, Mom, your grandson's up to his old capers. He never learns. This time he skipped school and got drunk." Broadcasting humiliation is another form of verbal abuse.

Indirect Verbal Abuse

Some forms of verbal abuse are more subtle, but they are just as hurtful. Among the best known forms of indirect abuse are sarcasm, teasing and subtle put-downs veiled in humor. A child is often unable to distinguish between this form of verbal abuse and the truth. As a result his defenses are down, and his exposed sense of self-worth is seared just like his back gets burned if he plays in the warm sunshine too long.

Some parents make cruel statements to their child, and then try to wriggle off the hook by saying, "I was only kidding." These parents use humor to dig into their children, often making them the butt of their jokes. They specialize in laughing at their children instead of with them. They criticize their child's characteristics, abilities or weaknesses by joking about them in public.

One father said about his child, "My son likes to play football. But you've never seen it played the way he plays it. It looks more like baseball." In each of his attempts to be funny (which often failed), this father shot a poison dart into the spirit of his child. Proverbs has something to say about this pattern too: "As a madman who casts firebrands, arrows and death, so is

---

Some parents make cruel statements to their child, and then try to wriggle off the hook by saying, "I was only kidding."

---

the man who deceives his neighbor and then says, Was I not joking?" (26:18,19). When humor becomes the camouflage for criticism, a toxic weapon is in use.

WORDS OF JUDGMENT

Let's consider now one of the more common toxic verbal weapons found in a parent's arsenal: words of judgment. Parents speak judgmentally for the purpose of controlling the child. But the usual effect is discouragement, dejection and reinforcement of the characteristic the parent actually wants to change. When you fire the guns of judgment, the child ends up overloaded with blame, making him feel unacceptable to you and to himself.

Belittling is one of the most damaging forms of judgment. A child is belittled when you make light of his behavior, feelings, thoughts or accomplishments.

Any kind of belittling conveys to the child: "Your feelings are no good. Your ideas are no good. Your behavior is no good." The bottom line of this message is an emotional time bomb: "You are no good."

A child will respond to belittlement by withdrawing from you in a number of ways. He may not listen to you, he may clam up and not share anything of substance with you or he may strike back in some less obvious way.

Blaming is another toxic verbal weapon of judgment. I've seen parents use this approach to avoid accepting responsibility for their own actions. They blame the child for "causing" their problems or emotional upsets. You've probably heard yourself or another parent say to a child:

- "You make me so upset."
- "Your behavior is going to be the death of me."
- "I wish you wouldn't make me so angry."

What they are actually saying is, "This wouldn't have happened if it hadn't been for you. You're responsible!" How can a child, who is less able to understand life and relationships than an adult, handle such a statement of blame?

Sometimes a parent blames a child for something he did well but could have done better. In these statements the parent hammers the child with shoulds and shouldn'ts:

- "You should have done it my way."
- "You should have been done sooner."
- "You shouldn't have worn your good clothes outside."

- "You shouldn't ever do that in this home."

What the parent is pointing out to the child may be valid. But a "should" is often a weapon of blame which wounds the child and reinforces the very behavior or attitude the parent is attempting to correct. A child translates "you should have" into "you did it wrong." Your purpose isn't to help him retain what he did wrong but to help him focus on what you want him to do. So instead of using "should" and "shouldn't," phrase your statement in a way which will leave a positive impression: "I appreciate what you did. Here's another way you might want to try next time."

FINDING FAULT

One of the most destructive forms of verbal abuse is fault-finding. It is another form of judgment. The fault-finding parent seems to have an insatiable need to point out the defects of his children. He's always looking at the child through a critical lens and pointing out what he did or didn't do, what he said or didn't say or what he might or might not do in the future. Even the most insignificant errors or defects are quickly exposed and corrected. Parents who are challenged about their fault-finding often respond defensively, "I'm just trying to save him from some painful mistakes later on in life." But the pain which the child experiences from consistent criticism and correction often outweighs the benefits.

Frequently the fault-finding parent is a perfectionist who holds the unrealistic expectation that his children ought to be perfect. This expectation is the trigger for verbal attacks and pressure when the child fails. Unfortunately, the child often becomes the scapegoat for the parent's failure to be perfect. But since he can't live up to his parent's expectation of perfection either, the child often becomes a procrastinator. His fear of failing to do things perfectly for Mom or Dad will prompt him to postpone the actions for which he will inevitably be criticized. The more he procrastinates, the more overwhelmed he feels by the pressure to perform. Soon he is immobilized by his lack of perfection and gives up. (If you would like additional information about perfectionism, see *Hope for the Perfectionist* [Thomas Nelson Publishers], by David Stoop, and *Healing Grace* [Victor Books], by David Seamands.)

Fault-finding is not always verbal. A sneering look, a frown or a condemning gesture also convey displeasure. Nonverbal put-downs are often difficult for a child to interpret. When the parent snaps impatiently, "You still didn't pick up all the toys in the yard," at least the child knows what the problem is. But a nonverbal criticism, such as an unexplained scowl or the silent treatment, leaves the child wondering. Silence is the classic form of control, punishment and criticism in a dysfunctional home. God did not put us into families to be silent. We were created to communicate with each other.

The Fallout of Fault-finding

Here are several reasons why fault-finding is so destructive in the parent-child relationship:

- Fault-finding deeply wounds the child. Constant verbal and nonverbal criticism says, "I don't accept you for who you are at this time in your life. You don't measure up, and I can't accept you until you do." In more than 25 years of counseling I have heard multitudes of people in my office cry out in pain, "My parents' criticism ripped me apart as a child. They made me feel like dirt. I never felt accepted, and I'm still looking for someone who will tell me I'm all right."

- Fault-finding also wounds the parent. The wounded child becomes afraid or angry and retaliates through overt or covert withdrawal, resentment or aggression.

- Fault-finding really doesn't change the child. Though the child may appear to change his behavior in response to parental criticism, his heart rarely changes. Some children simply learn to cover their rebellious attitude with external compliance.

- Fault-finding is contagious. A fault-finding parent teaches intolerance to the child by example. Thus the child learns to be critical and unaccepting of himself and others.

- Fault-finding accentuates negative traits and behaviors. When you pay undue attention to a child's mistakes or irresponsible behaviors, you tend to reinforce them instead of eliminate them.

Perhaps the following words, written by W. Livingston Larned to his own son, illustrate the negative impact of critical words:

FATHER FORGETS
Listen, son: I am saying this as you lie asleep, one little paw crumpled under your cheek and the blond curls stickily wet on your damp forehead. I

have stolen into your room alone. Just a few minutes ago, as I sat reading my paper in the library, a stifling wave of remorse swept over me. Guiltily I came to your bedside. These are the things I was thinking, son: I had been cross to you. I scolded you as you were dressing for school because you gave your face merely a dab with a towel. I took you to task for not cleaning your shoes. I called out angrily when you threw some of your things on the floor.

At breakfast I found fault, too. You spilled things. You gulped down your food. You put your elbows on the table. You spread butter too thick on your bread. And as you started off to play and I made for my train, you turned and waved a hand and called, "Good-bye, Daddy!" and I frowned, and said in reply, "Hold your shoulders back!"

Then it began all over again in the late afternoon. As I came up the road I spied you, down on your knees, playing marbles. There were holes in your stockings. I humiliated you before your boyfriends by marching you ahead of me to the house. Stockings were expensive—and if you had to buy them you would be more careful! Imagine that, son, from a father!

Do you remember, later, when I was reading in the library, how you came in timidly, with a sort of hurt look in your eyes? When I glanced up over my paper, impatiently at the interruption, you hesitated at the door. "What is it you want?" I snapped. You said nothing, but ran across in one tempestuous plunge, and threw your arms around my neck and kissed me, and your small arms tightened with an affection that God has set blooming in your heart and which even neglect could not wither. And then you were gone, pattering up the stairs.

Well, son it was shortly afterwards that my paper slipped from my hands and a terrible sickening fear came over me. What has habit been doing to me? The habit of finding fault, of reprimanding—this was my reward to you for being a boy. It was not that I did not love you; it was that I expected too much of youth. I was measuring you by the yardstick of my own years.

And there was so much that was good and fine and true in your character. The little heart of you was as big as the dawn itself over the wide hills. This was shown by your spontaneous impulse to rush in and kiss me good night. Nothing else matters tonight, son. I have come to your bedside in the darkness and I have knelt there, ashamed!

It is a feeble statement; I know you would not understand these things if I told them to you during your waking hours. But tomorrow I will be a real daddy! I will chum with you, and suffer when you suffer, and laugh when you laugh. I will bite my tongue when impatient words come. I will keep saying as if it were a ritual: "He is nothing but a boy—a little boy!"[1]

The Antidote to Finding Fault

How can you begin to reverse the destruction of fault-finding words and actions? By learning to love your children unconditionally. Years ago I came across some guidelines for unconditional love by Dr. Ross Campbell which spoke to me as a parent. I have shared them with other parents over the years. Perhaps they will speak to you as well.

How I wish I could say, "I love my children all the time regardless of anything else, including their behavior." But like all parents, I cannot; yet I will give myself credit for trying to arrive at that wonderful goal of loving them unconditionally. I do this by constantly reminding myself that:

a. They are children.
b. They will tend to act like children.
c. Much of childish behavior is unpleasant.
d. If I do my part as a parent and love them despite their childish behavior, they will be able to mature and give up their childish ways.
e. If I only love them when they please me (conditional love), and convey my love to them only during those times, they will not feel genuinely loved. This in turn will make them insecure, damage their self-image, and actually prevent them from moving on to better self-control and more mature behavior. Therefore, their behavior and development is my responsibility as much as theirs.
f. If I love them unconditionally, they will feel good about themselves and be comfortable with themselves.
g. If I only love them when they meet my requirements or expectations, they will feel incompetent. They will believe it is fruitless to do their best because it is never enough. Insecurity, anxiety, and low self-esteem will plague them. There will be constant hindrances in their emotional

and behavioral growth. Again, their total growth is as much my responsibility as theirs.

h. For my sake as a struggling parent, and for my sons' (and daughters') sakes, I pray my love for my children will be as unconditional as I can make it. The future of my children depends on this foundation.[2]

Yes, there are times when we need to give constructive guidance (that's my term for criticism). As a Christian parent, you are scripturally responsible to guide, teach, correct and discipline your children. You may even find it necessary to confront your children concerning irresponsible behavior such as lying, stealing, substance abuse, reckless driving, etc. *But how you express that corrective guidance makes all the difference in the world in how your child receives it!* Negative, fault-finding condemnation does not promote a child's inner growth. Furthermore, condemnation is not scriptural. Jesus said:

Do not judge and criticize and condemn others, so that you may not be judged and criticized and condemned yourselves. . . . In accordance with the measure you deal out to others it will be dealt out again to you" (Matt. 7:1,2).

Paul wrote:

Let us no more criticize and blame and pass judgment on one another, but rather decide and endeavor never to put a stumbling block or an obstacle or a hindrance in the way of a brother (Rom. 14:13).

All of our communication with our children, including constructive guidance, should be nurturing. Nurturing communication fosters a loving, trusting parent-child relationship. Nurturing words build, support, encourage and express caring. The child with fault-finding parents becomes the prisoner of his own negative feelings. But the child who grows up in an atmosphere of encouragement is released to develop emotionally and is open to experiencing God's grace.

Here's how several adults described the nurture they received from their parents:

- "Dad understood my feelings. He never put me down even when he didn't understand."
- "Mom listened to me and didn't judge me. She accepted me right where I was."
- "Dad always thought I was a winner. He believed in me even when I didn't believe in myself."
- "I got lots of encouragement. When I did something wrong, Dad never made me feel that I would do the same thing again. He believed that I could change!"
- "Mom had time for me, not just to give advice, but time just to chat with me. And she helped me figure out the problems for myself."
- "My folks were cheerleaders. I know I hurt them and disappointed them many times. But they stuck with me."
- "I don't think I ever heard a put-down from my folks."

DISMANTLING YOUR VERBAL ARSENAL

Perhaps you're thinking, "All right, Norm. You've made your point. But I still get frustrated with my kids at times. I want them to mind me. I want them to turn out right. How do I change my communication responses from abusive to nurturing?"

By asking for help you've taken the first step. Before you can make any changes, you must acknowledge your need to change. Congratulations—you're on your way!

The second step is to clearly identify the abusive patterns you are employing. To help you do so, I suggest that you do what I've asked numerous parents in my counseling office to do: Begin recording your con-

> ### All of our communication with our children, including constructive guidance, should be nurturing.

versations at home. Get a cassette recorder and several blank 90-minute tapes. Turn the recorder on at mealtimes, at the onset of a family argument or at other occasions when the family is together, and let it run. After a few self-conscious moments, everyone will forget about the recorder and begin to interact normally.

After you have recorded several interactions, listen to the tapes. As you listen, focus on your own communication patterns instead of judging other family members for their use of verbal weapons. Write down your abusive comments from the tape and summarize the kinds of toxic verbal weapons you use (sarcasm, teasing, fault-finding, blaming, belittling, etc.).

The third step is to begin integrating the guidance

of Scripture into your communication. Here's a practical way to do so:

- Write out each of the following verses about communication from Proverbs on a separate index card: 10:19; 12:18; 14:29; 16:24; 17:9; 19:11; 29:20.
- On the back of each card write a statement describing how you see yourself complying with that verse. Make it specific and personal, perhaps beginning with the words, "I will..."
- Carry the cards with you for the next 30 days, and read each verse and statement aloud several times a day. By the end of 30 days you will probably have memorized most of the verses and begun to integrate their concepts into your communication.

I have discovered that it is helpful to involve your spouse or a trusted friend in this process. Tell somebody what you are doing, read to them the statements you have written and ask them to hold you accountable to follow through with the exercise.

I also suggest that you keep a personal parent-child communication growth diary. Write down your progress in attitudes, feelings and communication daily. All entries must be positive; don't keep score of the problems or defeats. Note how you change and how your child responds to your changes. Share your responses with your spouse or another trusted friend. At the end of each week, reread the entire diary from the beginning. Keep your diary faithfully for one month, then decide if you want to continue for another month.

When you employ toxic verbal weapons in your communication, you are standing against your child. But when your words are full of nurture and encouragement, you are standing with him. First Thess. 5:11 states: "Therefore encourage one another and build each other up, just as in fact you are doing" (*NIV*). A child needs his parents to believe in his potential. Believe in your child. Focus on his resources to build his self-esteem, self-confidence and feelings of worth. Help your child see how God views him. Become a talent scout, helping your child discover his uniqueness, giftedness and potential. As a result, you may see your child respond in the way you desire. What have you got to lose?

FOR THOUGHT AND DISCUSSION

Share your responses with your spouse, a trusted friend or your study group.

1. What situations with your child provoke you to the kinds of verbal abuse you want to change? How does your child respond when you use your verbal weapons?

2. Which toxic verbal weapons do you find yourself using with your child? Circle the word for each weapon below which represents how frequently you use it in parent-child communication:

• Sarcasm

    Never   Almost never   Sometimes   Often   Very often

- Hurtful teasing

  Never   Almost never   Sometimes   Often   Very often

- Subtle put-downs

  Never   Almost never   Sometimes   Often   Very often

- Reminding the child of misbehavior

  Never   Almost never   Sometimes   Often   Very often

- Expressing joy in the child's discipline

  Never   Almost never   Sometimes   Often   Very often

- Projecting failure on the child

  Never   Almost never   Sometimes   Often   Very often

- Taking cheap verbal shots at the child

  Never   Almost never   Sometimes   Often   Very often

- Verbally kicking the child when he's down

  Never   Almost never   Sometimes   Often   Very often

- Verbal harassment

  Never   Almost never   Sometimes   Often   Very often

- Broadcasting the child's humiliation

  Never   Almost never   Sometimes   Often   Very often

- Belittling

  Never   Almost never   Sometimes   Often   Very often

• Blaming

Never   Almost never   Sometimes   Often   Very often

• Fault-finding

Never   Almost never   Sometimes   Often   Very often

3. What kind of attitude or mind set do you want toward your child? Attitude *is* a choice. Put a plus sign (+) beside each mind-set you want to develop and a minus sign (-) beside those which are undesirable to you.

• A mind-set to make my child feel bad.
• A mind-set to cut my child down to size.
• A mind-set to discipline, heal, forgive and reconcile.
• A mind-set to get back at my child.
• A mind-set to convince my child what a bad person he is.
• A mind-set to convince my child how much I believe in him.[3]

Notes
1. *How to Win Friends and Influence People* Copyright © by Dale Carnegie. Renewed © 1964 by Donna Dale Carnegie and Dorothy Carnegie. Reprinted by permission of SIMON & SCHUSTER, INC.
2. D. Ross Campbell, M.D., *How to Really Love Your Children* (Wheaton, IL: Victor Books, 1977), pp. 30,31. Used by permission.
3. Buddy Scott, *Relief for Hurting Parents* (Nashville: Oliver-Nelson, a division of Thomas Nelson Publishers, 1989), adapted from p. 84.

7

HOW TO FRUSTRATION-PROOF YOUR COMMUNICATION

I'LL never forget an experience with my daughter, Sheryl, that really taught me a lesson. One day I was in the garage trying to assemble a new item we had purchased for the home. I say "trying" because I'm not mechanically inclined; I'm all thumbs when it comes to putting things together. Besides, the assembly instructions for this device were confusingly technical, and the factory had shorted me two screws and a nut. I was getting frustrated and angry and was starting to mutter under my breath.

Just then Sheryl walked through the garage and asked what I was doing. "What does it look like I'm doing?" I growled. "I'm trying to put this dumb thing together. But the instructions could just as well be written in Chinese, and some numskull back at the factory doesn't know how to count screws and nuts."

"Daddy," Sheryl interrupted in the midst of my tirade, "just because you're frustrated about not being able to put that thing together, don't take out your anger on me." Then she turned and marched into the house.

I sat there with my mouth hanging open, stunned. She was right! A simple task had frustrated me, my frustration had boiled to anger, and I had vented my anger in unkind words to Sheryl and uncomplimentary words about the manufacturers of the device. I was ashamed of my response and later apologized to Sheryl for my hasty, unloving words.

Can you identify with my experience? Of course you can. You know what it's like to get frustrated and lash out at somebody with angry, hurtful words which you later regret. Often your children are both the source of your deepest frustrations and the target of your angry words. For example, you ask your child to be careful not to spill her chocolate milk on the clean tablecloth. But moments later you hear her call from the table, "Oops, I'm sorry, Mommy!" You turn to see a river of chocolate milk coursing across the tablecloth and cascading to the new carpet below. At that moment the doorbell rings signalling the arrival of your dinner guests. "Alyson, you are the clumsiest girl I've ever known!" you explode as you pull her off the chair and reach for the roll of paper towels. "Go to your room and get ready for bed!"

All it takes is one little incident to pull the trigger and the adrenaline begins to flow. You grit your teeth and clench your fists. Your muscles become taut, your stomach tightens and your heart rate accelerates. You are coiled and ready to react.

For a brief moment you try not to erupt. You know you should back off and cool down. But your child continues to ignore your instructions, and you suddenly lash out with a belittling comment of criticism

---

Frustration doesn't have to lead to an angry reaction. You are free to decide how you will respond to it.

---

and judgment. The words penetrate your child like bullets. They wound his heart. They crush his spirit. You are somewhat aware that you are hurting your child, but your mouth is already in gear and the cutting words you really don't want to say are rolling out.

Frustration, anger, wounding words: Unfortunately, we follow that three-step response all too often when our children misbehave, irritate us or fail to live up to our expectations. But I have good news for you. It doesn't have to be that way! You may not always be able to prevent your child's behavior from irritating you. But you can prevent the chain reaction which often results in words which wound your child's spirit.

Let me compare the process to firing a gun. When you pull the trigger, the firing pin ignites the gun powder in the shell which explodes and propels the bullet toward its target. If you remove the firing pin, you can still pull the trigger, but the gun won't go *bang* and nobody will get shot. Frustration is like the firing pin. Your child's attitude or behavior may pull your trigger, but if you deal with your frustration before it ignites into anger, you can keep yourself from exploding with hurtful words. This chapter is about resolving your frustration before it pollutes your communication with your child.

RESOLVING FRUSTRATION IS YOUR CHOICE

Frustration is defined as a sense of insecurity or dissatisfaction arising from unresolved problems or unfulfilled needs. Let's consider several points about the frustration you experience as a parent:

- You will at times become irritated, disappointed and frustrated with your children when they cause you problems, fail to fulfill your expectations or uncover your unmet needs.
- Frustration is a normal response. But you have a choice about how far your frustration will go and how you will deal with it.
- Anger is also a normal response. God created us with the capacity to experience anger. But how you handle your anger at your children is up to you, especially when it comes to communicating with them.
- Accepting and recognizing your frustration and anger is healthy. Denying or repressing them can be disastrous.

Most people respond to frustration and anger in one of several negative ways. Some people explode and give vent to their anger with destructive words or actions. Everyone around them feels the heat. The explosion may take the form of a direct verbal attack or an indirect, nonverbal killing look.

Other people repress and internalize their anger. Instead of exploding and hurting others, these people hold it all in and hurt themselves.

Still others express their anger in passive/aggressive ways like withholding love, giving the cold shoulder, belittling the individual in front of others, etc. They are indirect and underhanded, but the thrust of the anger is just as destructive.

A POSITIVE RESPONSE IS POSSIBLE

Many people feel that frustration automatically results in an expression of anger. That's a myth. It is possible to experience frustration as a parent without becoming upset and injuring your child with hurtful words. Frustration is a matter of attitude, thought and choice. Consider these words from a therapist who specializes in helping people deal with their frustrations:

> Millions of frustrations are far more easily tolerated than we usually think. Children not finishing their dinner is not an awful frustration, just the waste of a few cents. If a few cents bothers you, put the plate in the refrigerator until later. A person swerving in front of you in traffic is not doing something that calls for a nuclear explosion. It isn't awful to have someone honking his horn impolitely behind you—it's only slightly annoying. Not getting your raise can hurt your pocketbook, but not you—unless you let it. Frustrations are not usually earthshaking to begin with; they can be toler-

ated quite nicely if we make the effort. Secondly, frustrations, even if they are severe, don't have to lead to disturbances unless we allow them to.[1]

Frustration doesn't have to lead to an angry reaction. You are free to decide how you will respond to it. Problems, difficulties, disappointments, heartaches and failures are an unavoidable part of parenting. Your response to them—either anger or joy—is your choice!

I remember two events from the Olympic games in Montreal many years ago which illustrate the contrast between these two responses to frustration. In the two-man sailing event, the team from Britain came in 14th in a field of 16. The two British sailors were so frustrated by their performance that they set fire to their yacht and waded ashore while it went up in flames! Their response to frustration was destructive and costly.

Olneus Charles, a distance runner from Haiti, also experienced frustration in the Montreal Olympics. He was lapped nine times in the 10,000 meter race and came in dead last, five minutes behind everyone else. But he didn't become discouraged or quit. He chose not to let his frustrating experience get the best of him.

Your children will try your patience, irritate you and sometimes humiliate you in ways you never thought possible. But you can respond with words that heal instead of words that wound. It's your choice.

In his book *Parenting Isn't for Cowards*, Dr. James Dobson relates the frustrations shared by over 1,000 mothers and fathers. One of the delightful stories he received described a mother's first trip to the movies with her son.

I'll never forget the mother who had been cooped up with her toddler for several weeks. In a desperate effort to get out of the house, she decided to take her son to a Muppet movie . . . his first. As soon as they arrived in the theater, the mother discovered a minor technical problem. The child didn't weigh enough to keep the spring seat down. There was nothing left to do but hold this churning, squirming two-year-old on her lap throughout the movie.

It was a mistake. Sometime during the next two hours, they lost control of a large Pepsi and king-sized box of buttered popcorn! That gooey mixture flowed over the child onto the mother's lap and down her legs. She decided to sit it out since the movie was almost over. What she didn't know, unfortunately, was that she and her son were being systematically cemented together. When the movie was over, they stood up and the mother's wraparound skirt came unraveled. It stuck to the bottom of the toddler and followed him up the aisle! She stood there clutching her slip and thanking the Lord she had taken time to put one on![2]

Did God design parenting to be so frustrating? No. But He allows these daily challenges so you can develop flexibility and become all He wants you to be as a Christian parent. Resisting and fighting the normal upsets of parenting breeds frustration and anger. But optimistically anticipating and accepting upsets, changes, surprises and hurts will cause the reaction of angry, hurtful words to misfire. Remember: It's your choice!

How to Reduce Parental Frustration

I hear parents in my office and in my seminars say to me again and again, "Norm, I don't want to talk abusively to my kids, but something just comes over me and I let it rip! There's a limit to what I can take from them. I think I really love my children, but sometimes I don't like them very much. I've even had thoughts of throttling them! That scares me. I don't know what to do to change."

I usually respond with a question: "When you feel frustrated and angry with your children, what do you focus on: how they behaved and what you said or how you would like them to behave?"

They usually reply, "Oh, I keep mulling over their misbehavior and my destructive comments. I relive it again and again and beat up on myself for hurting them."

"Do you realize that by rehearsing your failures you are programming yourself to repeat them?" I ask.

They usually respond with quizzical looks. But it's true. When you spend so much time thinking about what you shouldn't have done, you reinforce it. Furthermore, spending all your time and energy mentally rehashing your failures keeps you from formulating what you really want to do. Redirecting your time and energy toward a solution will make a big difference in how you communicate with your child! Focus your attention on how you want to respond to your frustrations and you will experience change!

Let's consider several steps you can take to reduce your frustration as a parent and curb your hurtful words.

Be Honest and Accountable

The first step in dealing with your frustration is to find someone with whom you can share your parenting concerns and develop an accountability relationship. Select a person who will be willing to pray with you and check up on you regularly to see how you are doing. If you are working through these steps as a couple, ask another couple to keep you accountable. We all need the support and assistance of others.

You also need to be honest and accountable to yourself and to your spouse about the changes you want to make. Take a sheet of paper and respond in writing to the following questions. Then share your responses with your spouse or prayer partner:

- How do you feel about becoming frustrated? Be specific. How do you feel about getting angry? There are some people who enjoy their frustration and anger. It gives them an adrenaline rush and a feeling of power. Does this description fit you in any way?
- When you are frustrated, do you want to be in control of your response or be spontaneous? In other words, do you want to decide what to do or just let your feelings take you where they want to go?
- If you want to stay in control, how much time and energy are you willing to spend to make this happen? For change to occur, the motivational level needs to remain both constant and high.
- When you are bothered by something your child does, how would you like to respond? What would you like to say at that time? Be very specific.

Internalize the Guidelines from God's Word

There is a reason why God inspired men to write the Scriptures and why He preserved them through the centuries for us: God's guidelines for life are the best. Regardless of what you may have experienced or been taught in the past, God's plan works!

Write out each of the following verses from Proverbs on a separate index cards: 12:18; 14:29; 16:32. Add to your card file other Scriptures you discover which relate to frustration and anger. Read these verses aloud morning and evening for one month, and you will own them.

Plan Your Response to Frustration in Advance

You will only be able to change if you plan to change. Your intentions may be good, but once the frustration-anger sequence kicks into gear, your ability to think clearly is limited.

Identify in advance what you want to say to your child when you begin to feel frustrated. Be specific. Write out your responses and read them aloud to yourself and to your prayer partner. In my counseling office I often have clients practice their new responses on me, and I attempt to respond as the other person. By practicing on me they are able to refine their statements, eliminate their anxiety or feelings of discomfort and gain confidence for their new approach. Your spouse or prayer partner could assist you this way.

Learn to Delay Your Responses

Begin training yourself to delay your verbal and behavioral responses when you recognize that you are frustrated with your child. The Proverbs repeatedly admonish us to be slow to anger. You must slow down your responses if you want to change any habits of hasty, hurtful words you have cultivated over the years. When we allow frustration and anger to be expressed unhindered, they are like a runaway loco-motive. You need to catch them before they gather momentum so you can switch the tracks and steer them in the right direction.[3]

One helpful way to change direction is to use a trigger word. Whenever you feel frustration and anger rising within you, remind yourself to slow down and gain control by saying something to yourself like "stop," "think," "control," etc. Use a word that will help you switch gears and put your new plan into action.

Make Room for Your Child's Frustrating Behavior

One of the approaches I often suggest to parents to diffuse a frustrating power struggle with their children is this: Mentally give your child permission to be involved in the behavior which frustrates you. For example, your little Jennifer always leaves the back door open when she goes out to play—and it drives you up the wall. More than once you have angrily shouted after her, "Jenny, come back here this instant and close this door! You were not raised in a barn!" Often the skirmish over the back door has ruined the morning for both you and Jenny.

The next time she leaves the back door open, say to yourself, "I don't know why Jenny leaves the door open, but I'm not going to let it ruin my day. It's not the worst thing she could do. If she wants to leave the door open, I give her permission to do so. I know there is a reason for it, and it's important for me to discover that reason. It will be a learning experience for Jenny and me as we try to resolve this behavior."

The permission-giving approach defuses your frustration and gives you time to implement a level-headed plan.

Don't get me wrong; I'm not suggesting that you emotionally give up and allow your child to do anything he wants to do. There are some behaviors which are highly detrimental to the child which require a firm and immediate no! But with everyday behaviors which are more frustrating than dangerous, challenge yourself to quit fighting and go with the flow. By doing so you may be able to skirt your child's defenses and solve the problem without wounding him by coming unglued.

Many parents are skeptical when I suggest the permission-giving strategy. But they often come back after trying it and report amazing results. One mother said, "Norm, the first time I heard your suggestion, I thought you were crazy. But I tried it. I discovered that I was less frustrated. My posture was less rigid, and I was more relaxed as I dealt with my son. One day he said, 'Mom, you're doing something different. You're not getting so uptight, and you seem to be hearing what I say.' That was all the reinforcement I needed!"

Change Your Inner Conversation
Your inner conversation—also called self-talk—is where your frustrations are either tamed or inflamed. What you say to your children and how you behave toward them is determined by how you talk to yourself about their behaviors and responses. In fact, your most powerful emotions—anger, depression, guilt, worry—as well as your self-esteem as a person and a parent are initiated and fed by your inner conversa-

tion. Changing your inner conversation is essential to keeping your parenting frustrations from erupting into wounding words.

Just before leaving for his Saturday morning golf game, Art asked his 11-year-old son to clean up his room and wash the family car. Jimmy said he would. But when Art returned home, Jimmy was nowhere to

---

Coach yourself to think, "I'm taking some positive steps toward resolving my frustration and anger. This will really make a difference in my relationship with my child."

---

be seen. His room was only half clean, and the car was still a mess. Let's listen in on Art's inner conversation as he surveys the scene: "Where is that boy? He didn't follow my instructions. He's so lazy and inconsiderate. I give him everything, and he doesn't even have the courtesy to do a little work. He never follows through. Wait till I see him. And he always leaves without writing a note telling me where he's going. I'll ground that kid for a month!"

You may argue that Art had a right to be frustrated and angry. Maybe so, maybe not. Regardless, Art was free to choose how he thought about the scene before him. And his inner conversation reveals that he chose to fuel his frustration with distorted thinking. He resorted to *labeling*, calling Jimmy lazy and inconsiderate. Labeling encourages frustration because it perpetuates a negative view. You begin to look for behaviors in your child which reinforce the labels you have attached to him. You tend to overlook the positives and look for the worst.

Another evidence of Art's distorted thinking is *magnification*. Words like "never," "always" and "every" magnify occasional misbehaviors into lifetime habits. Magnifying the child's misbehavior only serves to intensify parental frustration.

Art's inner conversation was based on hasty, negative assumptions. Perhaps an emergency in the neighborhood called Jimmy away from his task. Perhaps an out-of-town relative arrived unexpectedly and took Jimmy to the mall for the afternoon. Perhaps a shut-in down the street called Jimmy to run an important errand. Maybe he left a note explaining his whereabouts, but Art was so busy thinking the worst that he didn't look for it. You will save yourself a lot of frustration and anger if you learn to base your inner conversations on hard facts and positive assumptions.

God's Word has a lot to say about how we think. If you have difficulty with negative inner conversations, I suggest that you write out the following Scriptures on index cards and begin reading them aloud to yourself every morning and evening: Isa. 26:3; Rom. 8:6,7; 2 Cor. 10:5; 12:2; Eph. 4:23; Phil. 4:6-9; 1 Pet. 1:13. If you would like further help on the topic of your inner conversation, see chapters 11 and 12 in *How to Speak Your Spouse's Language* (Fleming H. Revell), by this author. The principles suggested there for husbands and wives will also apply to parent-child relationships. Your thoughts can change if you choose to change them.

Adopt a Hopeful Attitude

If you approach these steps thinking, "This will never work," you have set yourself up for a failure. Instead, coach yourself to think, "I'm taking some positive steps toward resolving my frustration and anger. This will really make a difference in my relationship with my child. I know my communication with him will improve as I take these steps of growth."

To help you to develop a positive attitude, take a minute to list the advantages of being frustrated and the advantages of not being frustrated. Compare the two lists. Which results do you want? You are more likely to achieve these result by following the steps above.

A Record of Progress

Keep a record of your progress by maintaining a frustration diary in a small notebook. Keep your notebook handy at all times so you can write down your responses to your parenting frustrations. Share your entries with your spouse or prayer partner, but not with your children.

The purpose of this diary is two-fold. First, it will help you arrest your frustrations as they arise so you can control them instead of allowing them to control you. Second, it will help you plan a healthy, controlled response to future frustrations.

Here's a pattern for your frustration diary entries:

- The date and time the frustration occurred:
- The level of my frustration on a scale of 0 (none) to 10 (intense) was. . .
- My frustration was directed toward. . .

- Inside I felt . . .
- My inner conversation about my child and his behavior could be summarized:
- My verbal response to my child was . . .
- Did I move from frustration to anger? If so, what was the intensity of my anger?
- How did my response this time improve from the previous frustration experience?
- What would I like to feel and say at the next incident of frustration?
- What improvement will I make at the next incident of frustration?

Here's an example of how one woman—30-year-old Janice, mother of two preschoolers—charted her progress in her frustration diary:

- The date and time the frustration occurred: *Wednesday, February 6, at 11:30 A.M., just before lunch time.*
- The level of my frustration on a scale of 0 (none) to 10 (intense) was...*an 8!*
- My frustration was directed toward...*my five-year-old Stacy.*
- Inside I felt...*really irritated. In fact, I was ready to go over and grab her.*
- My inner conversation about my child and her behavior could be summarized: *That child is so stubborn. She doesn't listen to me. Her behavior is so selfish. I wonder how anyone can stand her when she's like that.*
- My verbal response to my child was: *"Stacy, you're impossible. You know you heard me. At times you are so bad!"*

- Did I move from frustration to anger? If so, what was the intensity of my anger? *You bet it did! I was upset, and my anger rose to about level 8 also.*
- How did my response this time improve from the previous frustration experience? *I'm not sure it did. It may have been louder. But I don't think it lasted as long this time, so I guess I could call that an improvement.*
- What would I like to feel and say at the next incident of frustration? *I don't want to feel irritated and angry. I guess I would like to talk to her in a firm, calm voice, but also get through to her.*
- What improvement will I make at the next incident of frustration? *I think I need to figure that out more in detail now. I'm going to memorize Prov. 12:18; 14:29; and 16:32. Then I'm going to write out and practice exactly what I will say when Stacy doesn't mind me. I'm also going to discuss and role-play the situation with my prayer partner.*

I'm going to use the "conscious delay principle." I will stop for a few seconds and remember what I want to say and do. In fact, in my mind I'm going to say, "It's all right for this to be happening. Most of her misbehavior isn't dangerous or life-threatening to her, and it's not the end of the world for me."

Then I am going to go to Stacy, kneel down to her level, put my hand gently on her shoulder, look her in the eye and in a calm voice ask, "What did I just tell you to do?"

This approach may make a difference.

Janice's approach, carefully planned and written in her diary, *did* make a difference.

I hope you truly believe that you can change your

responses to the frustrations you face. God believes you can. He is the one who can support you in your journey of change. Allow your spouse and your friends to help and support you also. Above all, believe that you can change and that your change will make a difference in your parent-child communication.

FOR THOUGHT AND DISCUSSION

Share your responses with your spouse, a trusted friend or your study group.

1. On a scale of 0 (desperate improvement needed) to 10 (no improvement needed), rate your present success at implementing each of the seven steps to reducing parental frustration.

• Be honest and accountable

    0 1 2 3 4 5 6 7 8 9 10

• Internalize the guidelines from God's Word

    0 1 2 3 4 5 6 7 8 9 10

• Plan your response to frustration in advance

    0 1 2 3 4 5 6 7 8 9 10

• Learn to delay your responses

    0 1 2 3 4 5 6 7 8 9 10

- Make room for your child's frustrating behavior

  0   1   2   3   4   5   6   7   8   9   10

- Change your inner conversation

  0   1   2   3   4   5   6   7   8   9   10

- Adopt a hopeful attitude

  0   1   2   3   4   5   6   7   8   9   10

2. Practice using the frustration diary by filling in the sample page below as it relates to the last incident of frustration you remember experiencing with your child.

- The date and time the frustration occurred:

- The level of my frustration on a scale of 0 (none) to 10 (intense) was . . .

- My frustration was directed toward . . .

- Inside I felt . . .

- My inner conversation about my child and his behavior could be summarized:

• My verbal response to my child was . . .

• Did I move from frustration to anger? If so, what was the intensity of my anger?

• How did my response this time improve from the previous frustration experience?

• What would I like to feel and say at the next incident of frustration?

• What improvement will I make at the next incident of frustration?

Notes
1. Paul A. Hauck, *Overcoming Frustration and Anger* (Philadelphia: Westminster Press, 1974), p. 65. Used by permission.
2. James C. Dobson, *Parenting Isn't for Cowards* (Dallas, Texas: WORD Incorporated, 1989), p. 11.
3. Neil Clark Warren, *Make Anger Your Ally* (Garden City, NJ: Doubleday and Co., 1983), adapted from p. 169.

8

MESSAGES THAT DISCOUNT, MESSAGES THAT NURTURE

ONE of our goals as parents should be to enable our children to think as highly of themselves as God thinks of them. A chief means for accomplishing this goal is the nurturing messages we convey, both verbally and nonverbally. If we fill their lives with positive messages of their value to us and to God, they will develop self-worth and self-discipline and become responsible, independent adults. Ideally, parent-child communication is filled with messages that nurture.

Unfortunately, however, we also send other kinds of messages to our children which not only fail to nurture them but negatively influence them from thinking of themselves as God thinks. These are messages that discount. Normally, the word discount has a pleasant ring to it. We like discount outlets which allow us to buy good merchandise at discounted prices. We enjoy getting early-bird menu discounts at our favorite restaurants. And some of us receive a substantial employee discount on goods or services where we work. But messages that discount are far from pleasant for us or for our children. They are destructive.

DISCOUNTING MESSAGES ARE NO BARGAIN

A discounting message reduces the value of the person to whom it is sent. When you send discounting messages to your children, you are not nurturing them toward self-worth; you are communicating to them in a way that causes them to doubt their value to you and to God.

At the heart of every discounting message is denial in one or more of the following areas:

- Many discounting messages deny the *existence* of a child or something he values or fears. When you ignore your child in some way you are sending a discounting message which denies his existence. When your daughter talks to her doll as if it is alive, and you say, "Why are you talking to Betsy? It's only a doll," you are denying the existence of her harmless fantasy. Or if she says she is afraid to be alone in her dark bedroom at night, and you say, "There's nothing to be afraid of," you are denying the existence of a problem which is very real to her.

- Some discounting messages deny the *severity* of a problem or the *importance* of an event in a child's life. For example, if your son is stressed out about completing a science project for school, and you convey, "It's no big deal," or choose to watch football instead of help him, you are denying the severity of his problem and the importance of his project.
- Other discounting messages deny the *solvability* of a problem a child is facing. You discount your child when you make statements like, "Forget it, Johnny, there's nothing you can do about it" or "College will be too difficult for you, so don't plan on it."
- Finally, some discounting messages deny the child's *ability* to succeed in some area. This message is conveyed when you refuse to take your son to soccer try-outs because "you'll never make the team anyway" or when you won't let your daughter help you with car repairs because "girls can't do mechanical things."

When you deny your child in any of these four areas, you are sending a discounting message that is counterproductive to the development of his maturity and independence.

Discounting During Crisis

Parents are often guilty of sending discounting messages during times of crisis in the child's life. One of the greatest gifts we can give our children is the ability to handle loss. Grieving is a part of life. But often a child's crisis experiences are minor in comparison to adult crises, so we tend to express messages of denial instead of nurture the child through the experience. In doing so we discount the child and hinder his growth.

Nine-year-old Sammy's dog has just died, and the boy is understandably grief-stricken. But his father discounts him by denying the existence of the crisis: "Sammy, stop crying. It was just a dog, and you didn't

---

Laughing *with* a child is usually healthy. But laughing *at* your child's pain, failure or embarrassment sends him a discounting message.

---

even have him very long." Or he may deny the severity of the crisis by saying, "It was just a dog, and there are lots of dogs just like him. Next week we'll go to the animal shelter and find one that's even better." Or he may deny the solvability of the crisis by saying, "Crying about it won't help at all. Every dog you have will eventually die, so you'd better get used to it." Or he may deny the boy's ability to succeed as a pet owner by saying, "If you'd only taken better care of your dog this wouldn't have happened. I'm not sure you deserve another dog."

During his time of crisis, Sammy desperately needs messages from his father which acknowledge his grief and the severity of his problem and affirm his ability to deal with it. Sammy's father could have said, "I know you're sad because your dog meant a lot to you. I can see the sadness in your eyes. I'm sad too. We will both miss him." This is a message that nurtures instead of discounts. We'll discuss nurturing messages in greater detail later in this chapter.

Fourteen-year-old Denise comes home from school in tears, devastated because she failed to be selected as a cheerleader. Her mother says, "Come on, Denise. You're carrying on as if your life is ruined. It's not the end of the world." In this message Denise is being discounted because her mother is denying the existence and severity of her crisis. "Staying in your room and crying all evening isn't going to help," her mother continues. "And there's nothing you can do about not making the squad, so snap out of it." This discounting message is blocking Denise's ability to solve her problem.

Denise needs a nurturing message during her crisis. After the initial grief subsided, Denise's mother should continue to nurture her by suggesting alternative involvements at school to help Denise grow through her disappointment at not being named a cheerleader.

Discounting Through Laughter

Another way we parents send discounting messages to our children is through laughter. Laughing *with* a child is usually healthy. But laughing *at* your child's pain, failure or embarrassment sends him a discounting message. It's another form of verbal abuse. Funny things happen in families. But if your child's misfortune is the source of the humor, you must wait to laugh until he laughs, even if it means biting your lip or leaving the room to control yourself.

There were some times when I blew it. I remember a vivid incident when Sheryl was twenty. She had come to our home for Easter dinner, and it was a day when nothing had gone right for her. She arose early, washed her hair and, since she had time left over, decided to wash out the bathtub. But when she turned the water on...you guessed it. The shower was on instead of the tub and it doused her hair. She had to repeat the process.

On the way to our house, the brakes went out on Sheryl's car. As we ate our meal, we were looking forward to our dessert—fresh ripe strawberries a friend had given to me. As Sheryl bit into this huge strawberry, she looked at the half that was in her hand and noticed something wiggling. She looked closer and discovered her worst bug enemy—an earwig. Somehow a family of the intrepid insects had burrowed into the core of the strawberry and set up shop. She shuddered and screamed and then realized she still had half of the berry in her mouth. She pulled it out and discovered half of another earwig. At that point, she lost control and went crying and screaming to the bathroom to wash her mouth out with soap and water. I lost it too, but I was rolling with laughter.

In fact, as I write this I discover that I am grinning and chuckling all over again. At the time, Sheryl was not pleased that I was laughing, but after awhile we were all laughing together. It's provided us with a great memory even though it was traumatic at the time. I am glad that she was twenty and not a young child when that happened, or I'd have been in even deeper trouble. If you do "lose it" and laugh, knowing it isn't best, an apology and explanation can help when the child has recovered his composure.

The Many Forms of Discounting

There are numerous other ways by which we send discounting messages to our children. Each of them reflects one or both of the recurring themes which are often prevalent in families where discounting occurs: criticism and abandonment. Notice also how the thread of denial is woven into each statement. Each of these discounting messages blinds the child to the truth of his value to God and hinders the development of his self-worth.

Abuse. Abuse in any form—physical, emotional, verbal, sexual—sends a clear discounting message to the child: "I don't like you the way you are. Your needs are not important to me." Many parents who would never think of abusing their children physically or sexually are surprised at how subtly verbal abuse invades their parent-child communication. Yet verbal abuse can be as discounting as other more obvious forms of abuse.

Neglect. Withholding attention physically, emotionally or verbally is a passive form of abuse. Neglect causes the child to feel abandoned. The discounting message he receives is, "You and your needs are not important. You don't deserve my attention."

Conditional love. Messages of conditional love are either subtle or blatant threats based on a parent's needs or expectations instead of the child's needs. The discounting message the child receives is, "I have value, but you don't. Your needs and feelings are not as important as mine. You must earn my love by fulfilling my expectations."

Indulgence. Parental acts of indulgence are forms of love which are overdone and even patronizing to the child. They are discounting messages because they foster in the child an unrealistic dependency on his parents, block his ability to think for himself and obscure the meaning of personal responsibility.

VICTIMIZING CHILDREN THROUGH DISCOUNTING MESSAGES

We hear so much about victimization today—citizens victimized by criminals, spouses victimizing each other in marriages, etc. Many of our children grow up feeling victimized because of the discounting messages they receive from their parents. I hear about parental victimization from adult children constantly in my counseling. One middle-aged woman told me, "I felt victimized most of my life. Oh, nothing dramatic happened to me when I was a child. I wasn't physically or sexually abused. But my mother was critical of me so much of the time. And whenever she said something nice, I couldn't believe it because her compliments were surrounded by so many discounting statements. Dad just wasn't available to me. He didn't want to talk or play with me. He was around physically, but I felt emotionally abandoned. I grew up wondering what was so wrong with me to keep him from being part of my life."

Children who grow up receiving discounting messages suffer from what we may call internalized victim blame. They learn to cope by blaming themselves for the criticism, abandonment and discounting messages they receive. By the time they reach adolescence and adulthood, they may be relatively free from their parents' discounting messages. But they have internalized blame to such an extent that they now discount themselves. They make statements of denial, criticism and blame to themselves like: "I should have been able to see that"; "What a dummy! I should have done that differently"; "There must be something wrong with me if the teacher has to show me the same formula over and over."

We parents sometimes unknowingly set the stage for internalized victim blame in our children through our discounting messages. We have no idea how powerfully our words, tone and actions influence our children. When we deny their existence, the severity or importance of their life events, the solvability of their problems or their ability to succeed, they internalize it and grow up discounting themselves in these areas. When we criticize them or abuse them verbally or nonverbally, they internalize it and grow up criticizing and abusing themselves.

Here are several common examples of discounting messages which lead to internalized victim blame in our children. Can you identify the denial, criticism, abandonment and abuse in these examples?

- Your child is selecting something at the store to buy with his allowance. You keep saying, "Are you *sure* that's what you want? Once you buy it, we're not bringing it back."
- You make fun of your child for being afraid of a large dog.
- You berate your child for losing a fish as he was trying to pull it into the boat.
- You tell your child, "You're going to turn out just like your rotten father."
- You ridicule your adolescent son for being bashful around girls.
- You make fun of your child's visible handicap or weakness in front of other children or your adult friends.

- You tell your six-year-old, "I will love you if you're a good boy."
- You say to your child, "If you get good grades and are quiet around the house, Daddy and I won't fight as much."
- You tell your 14-year-old, "I don't have time for you when you behave this way. Go to your room until you figure out what's wrong with you."[1]

A child who grows up on a steady diet of these kinds of messages will internalize an incredible knack for blaming himself for situations which are not his responsibility. Instead of becoming a mature, independent, self-confident individual, his adult life will be marked by self-blame, self-doubt, insecurity and feelings of victimization.

BREAKING THE DISCOUNTING CYCLE

As we have discussed messages that discount our children, do you find yourself described in the examples above? Have you identified yourself as a discounting parent? Before we turn our focus to the kinds of messages we should be giving our children—messages that nurture, we must talk about the source of the discounting messages you have been conveying. If you fail to acknowledge and deal with the source, your efforts to change your parent-child communication will be feeble at best.

If you are the conveyor of discounting messages to your children, it's very likely that you were the recipient of discounting messages from your parents as a child. To some degree you internalized victim blame and adopted a discounting self-attitude. Since a discounting attitude prevailed in your parents and now prevails in you, you in turn are passing along discounting messages to your children, who are internalizing victim blame as you did. Discounting in families is a vicious cycle. In order to stop the flow discounting messages from you to your children, you must break the cycle by dealing with your own discounting attitude.

The first step in breaking the cycle is to become aware of your discounting thought patterns. Do you ever deny the existence or severity of a problem in your life? Do you ever deny the solvability—or your ability to solve—a personal problem? Are you overly self-critical? Do you blame yourself for situations which are not your responsibility? Do you abuse yourself in any fashion?

The discounting tendency is often so ingrained that it is an automatic response. Bringing it to the surface will take some work on your part, but the results will be well worth it. Realize that you are not doing this to increase your guilt or to be hard on yourself. You are simply trying to discover how much of your behavior is motivated by personal discounting.

One way to determine if discounting is a part of your life is to keep track of your responses to problems. Ask yourself several times a day: Am I ignoring a problem which really exists? Am I pretending that the problem isn't as serious as it really is? Am I overreacting to the problem? Do I assume that there is no solution to the problem? Have I asked for help in solving the problem? Did I avoid the situation because I didn't think I could solve it?

The good news about discounting is that you can change; you can break the cycle in your family. You must become an explorer of your own attitudes and responses. Once you identify your discounting patterns, you are free to choose alternative nurturing approaches or solutions. What you learn about yourself will help you change your discounting responses toward your children.[2]

NURTURING MESSAGES PAY DIVIDENDS

Nurturing messages are those which convey to the child something good about himself. These positive messages don't increase the child's value; he is already priceless in God's eyes. But nurturing messages increase your child's value *in his own eyes*, thus opening the door for learning, growth, maturity and independence.

We need to nurture our children every day. Casual, spontaneous comments and planned, direct, eye-to-eye statements are equally effective. Nurturing involves giving more affirmations than corrections. Keep a written account of your messages to your child for a few days to see to which side the scale is tipped. If you make a point to share nurturing messages every day, it will soon become an automatic response.

Nurturing shows that you believe in your child's capacity to learn, change and grow. Nurturing shows that you are aware of the kind of picture you want your child to have of himself. Your child's mind is like a computer. Every message you send him goes into one of two files: discounting or nurturing. And the file with the most data will direct how your child sees himself and feels about himself. When nurturing is occurring on a regular basis, victim blame can't gain a foothold in your child's life.

Messages which nurture are based on unconditional love, which must be worked at, especially if you came from a discounting family instead of a nurturing family. But you can rely on Jesus Christ to fill the void in your life with His presence and help you learn how to love unconditionally as He loves us.

Let's look at two types of nurturing messages which will help develop healthy, self-disciplined children. The first category is affirmation and compliments for your child's good behavior and right choices. The second category is nurturing messages of correction of bad behavior and wrong choices.

Accentuating the Positive

It is easier for most parents to affirm positive behavior than to deal with negative behavior in a positive way. But we must continually remind ourselves to convey nurturing affirmations and compliments, such as:

- You treat your friends very nicely.
- You have a wonderful ability with tools.
- Thanks for doing such a good job on your chores today.
- Your schoolwork has really improved.
- I liked the way you cleaned your room. Thank you.
- You're a very special person to me.
- I'm so glad you're my child.
- I love you because you deserve to be loved. You don't have to earn it.
- You make my life more complete just by being you.
- I'm glad I have you. You teach me so much about life.

Such affirmations cause the child to realize, "Mom and Dad really love me. They think I'm a lovable person. My needs are important to them. They want to help me face the problems of life and solve them. What happens to me is very important to them. They trust me to think for myself and make good decisions."

> We don't correct our children to make them feel bad, but to help them discover a better way to do something.

As you convey nurturing messages, be sure your value judgments are attached to the child's behavior instead of his person. For example, a toddler exploring the family room approaches the television, which is within his reach. Fascinated by the shiny knobs and switches, he reaches out to touch the TV. His mother says, "Don't touch, Joshua. Remember: I said you can look at the television, but you can't touch it. Here are some other things you can touch." She jiggles a box of toys. Joshua stands in front of the TV for a moment wrestling with the temptation. Then he turns away toward the toys.

What would you have said to affirm Joshua? Many of us would remark, "Good boy, Joshua!" And if he had touched the TV against his mother's wishes, it would be, "Bad boy, Joshua!" But those kinds of statements are value judgments on Joshua. He soon learns that he is sometimes good and sometimes bad, which confuses his self-perception.

Instead, Joshua's mother said, "Good *choice*, Joshua!" She wants him to learn that he is capable of making good choices, for which he is affirmed, and bad choices, for which he is corrected. But Joshua is always regarded and nurtured as a good boy. This subtle but important distinction can make a world of difference in your child's self-image.

Dealing with the Negative

When our children make wrong choices or misbehave, they need to be corrected. But since we are concerned with nurturing them at all times, corrective messages must be delivered in a positive, affirmative way. We don't correct our children to make them feel bad, but to help them discover a better way to do something. Here are a few examples of nurturing statements of correction:

- Here is a way you can do it that you might like better.
- It sounds like it's hard for you to accept a compliment. Perhaps you need more practice accepting them, and I need more practice giving them.
- I'm not sure you heard what I said. Tell me what you heard, and then let me repeat what I said if you heard differently.
- Listen to the help and care I'm giving you right now.
- You can't do that any longer, but you can do this instead.
- That was a poor choice you made, but I have

some good ideas you may want to consider for getting back on track.

• You're not paying attention. Something must be on your mind, since you are so good at listening and thinking. I wonder what it is.

Whenever you must tell your child to "stop it," be sure to include in your message what the child may do instead. If you don't add some positive suggestions, your correction will be seen as negative criticism. It may stop the child from a hurtful or destructive activity, but it fails to build his self-discipline and confidence in an alternative area.

Share your messages of correction in a tone of voice that reflects your care and concern. Our tone has five times the impact as our words. Also, convey corrective messages with an affirmative touch on the hand or shoulder or a hug. Your nonverbal affirmations will convey your love and care even in an uncomfortable confrontation.

As you learn to nurture your children through positive verbal and nonverbal messages, they will feel comforted, loved and helped. To be most effective, your nurturing messages must be freely given and specifically tailored to meet the unique needs of each child. Each comment must be appropriate to the child and to the setting; not overdone or underdone.

What's the payoff? Your nurturing efforts will promote maturity and independence in your child by helping him think and do for himself. As you nurture your children through childhood and adolescence into adulthood, you will have the satisfaction of knowing that you helped them succeed at caring for themselves.[3]

FOR THOUGHT AND DISCUSSION

Share your responses with your spouse, a trusted friend or your study group.

1. Have you conveyed discounting messages—verbal or nonverbal—to your child in one or more of the following categories? Summarize your message and your child's response in each applicable category:

• Discounting in time of crisis or grief
   My message:

   My child's response:

• Discounting through laughter
   My message:

   My child's response:

• Discounting through some form of abuse
   My message:

   My child's response:

• Discounting through neglect
   My message:

   My child's response:

• Discounting through conditional love
   My message:

   My child's response:

- Discounting through indulgence
  My message:

  My child's response:

2. Did you come from a discounting family? If so, describe the kinds of discounting messages you parents conveyed to you. How have you perpetuated the cycle in your own attitude and your current family?
3. Answer the following questions as a first step in applying the concepts of nurturing from this chapter to your role as a parent:

- What kinds of nurturing messages do I want to convey to my child?

- What do I want my nurturing messages to accomplish?

- How do I want my child to feel as a result of my nurturing?

- What do I want my child to think as a result of my nurturing?

Notes
   1. Jean Illsley Clarke and Connie Dawson, *Growing Up Again* (New York: Harper and Row, 1989), adapted from pp. 17-27.
   2. Ibid., adapted from pp. 79-97.
   3. Ibid., adapted from pp. 53-61.

Part III

TAILOR-MADE COMMUNICATION TO FIT YOUR CHILD

9
EVERY CHILD IS A PRICELESS ORIGINAL

WE recently moved Christian Marriage Enrichment into new offices. Just before we moved in, the owners of the building recarpeted the complex. But for some reason the initial carpet order was 20 yards short, so new carpet was laid in all the rooms except one until the second order arrived two week later.

When the final 20 yards were laid, I noticed something interesting. The carpet was the same brand, the same design and the same color, but it was just a shade off from matching the original order. When I asked the installer about it, he said that the dye lots of the two orders were different. "Even though the company attempts to match the colors exactly when they mix a batch of new dye," he explained, "the dye lots are always just slightly different. It isn't noticeable until you put the two carpets side by side."

My experience with the carpets made me think how children in the same family can be so different. They are born to the same parents, raised in the same home and fed the same food, yet no two children—including identical twins—are completely alike. The biological, neurological and metabolic make-up of each child is unique. The intellectual potential of each is different. Why? Because the combination of physical characteristics inherited from each parent is a bit different for each child. Furthermore, the family environment is different for each succeeding child born to the same parents. The first child is born into a family of two members: mother and father. The second child is born into a family of three: mother, father and older brother or sister. The family dynamics change with each new member.

Successive children in the same family are also different because the parents are continually changing. With each addition to the family Mom and Dad are older, hopefully wiser, either more or less financially stable and at different stages in their personal development. In addition, each child is stamped with God's unique design, making him different from every other child ever born.

KEY TO COMMUNICATION: DISCOVERING EACH CHILD'S UNIQUENESS

In order to understand your children better, appreciate them more and communicate with them effectively, it is very important that you discover each child's uniqueness. Both you and your children will realize many benefits from your efforts to understand and accept their differences.

1. The first benefit is one you will appreciate: *Your level of parenting frustration will be diminished, and your peace of mind and ability to cope with each child's idiosyncrasies will increase.* The better you understand your child, the more likely the conflict level between you and your child will be reduced.

2. The development of each child will be enhanced. When you understand each child's uniqueness, you can be a greater support to all your children as they progress through each developmental stage.

3. When you are aware of each child's uniqueness, you can plan play activities that are appropriate to their social development. One activity may help one child develop socially while hindering another's development. What one child enjoys another finds boring. Some children work best being involved with others, and some work best by themselves. Knowing your child's social style will help you accommodate his social needs.

4. When you understand each child's uniqueness, you can discover their different learning styles. Some children learn because they like the learning experience. Others learn in order to apply what they learn to life situations. Still others have little interest in learning and need outside motivation. Understanding each child's learning style will not only facilitate meeting their educational needs but assist you in communicating with them in effective ways.[1] We'll talk more about different learning styles later in the chapter.

5. Knowing the uniqueness of each child will help you adjust your communication style to match each of theirs. For example, if one child is overwhelmed by receiving too many details at one time, you will know to share information with him in smaller chunks over a period of time. Or if a child responds more to facts than feelings, you will know to give him facts. Tailoring your communication style to each child will ensure that they both hear and understand you.

6. *Your awareness of each child's uniqueness will equip you for one of your most important tasks as a parent: affirming your children.* As children compare themselves with one another, they tend to focus their thinking on the qualities they don't have instead of the qualities they do have. They need to hear from you again and again in a positive way how special they are.

For example, seven-year-old John fails in his attempt to assemble a model airplane. He says to his father, "I give up. I can't do anything right."

Dad responds, "You know John, sometimes I feel that way too. But I've been watching you, and I think you can do lots of things well."

"What do you mean?"

"Well, you're the one in our family who shows care and concern for us and the pets. You always ask Mom and I how we're feeling, and you make little cards for us when we're not feeling well. You're so gentle and patient with Muffy and Chipper, and you always make sure they have enough food and water in their dishes. I think those are some of the many things you do well."

When you affirm a child's uniqueness, be sure you document your comments with specific examples of the quality you are affirming as John's father did. Also, it's important to help each child become aware of and appreciate the unique value of other family members. For example, John's father may add to his affirmation of John, "Mom and I also appreciate all the ideas and information that June shares with the family. You and your sister are both very special."

As parents affirm each child's uniqueness, the children will find it easier to believe that God accepts them just as they are.

It takes a tremendous amount of time, wisdom and

As parents affirm each child's uniqueness, the children will find it easier to believe that God accepts them just as they are.

---

prayer to recognize and affirm the uniqueness of each child and help each one develop his unique traits and abilities. But many parents don't realize how vital this process is to the child! A 20-year study of the behavioral development of 231 infants by Drs. Chess and Thomas emphasizes the importance. The study revealed that the interaction between parent and child affects how the child's unique abilities develop and how much tension exists between them. In her book *Your Child Is a Person*, Dr. Stella Chess reveals the key factor to a successful parent-child relationship is:

> The goodness of fit between the parents and child. If the parent's expectations and demands were in accord with the child's own capacities and style of behavior, then the child enjoyed optimal

development. If the parents didn't understand or appreciate a child's special qualities, problems did occur. Surprisingly, even divorce or the death of a parent was not as important as this basic "fit."[2]

HOW TO UNDERSTAND YOUR CHILD'S UNIQUENESS

How can parents discover their child's uniqueness? The best response I can give is wait, watch and listen, and keep track of your observations and discoveries. Ask yourself questions about your child, especially in the categories discussed below.

Discover What Motivates Your Child

What causes your child to move into action? Is he pushed from the inside or pulled from the outside? Does his energy come from within himself or from other persons and situations? Some children are pushed into action by their own ideas; they don't need any outside assistance. Other children are pulled into action by other people or some other outside factors. If you are going to understand your child's uniqueness and communicate with him effectively, you must learn what motivates him.

If your child is self-motivated, what forces are at work within him to move him to action? Here are several possibilities to explore:

- Creative ideas which have germinated.
- Concepts which have percolated in his mind.
- An imagination which has formed compelling ideas.
- Fantasies seeking translation into reality.
- Values or principles seeking application.

- Logical ideas pressing to be executed.
- Intuitive perceptions which can be applied.
- Convictions to be expressed.
- Other?

Communicating with a self-motivated child is an art. It requires that you frame your statements as possibilities and suggestions instead of telling. This child responds better to subtle, indirect guidance than to direct information and instruction. Plant ideas in his mind with comments like: "Could it be that you...?"; "Have you considered...?"; "What do you think would happen if...?"; "Did you see the article which suggested...?" You will be surprised what your self-motivated child can do with a few well-placed hints.

If your child is pulled into action by other people, under which of the following conditions does he most readily respond?

- A leader (teacher, friend, parent, peer) presents an opportunity.
- A leader presents conditions to be met.
- An authority or expert invites response.
- An inspiring person calls for commitment.
- A mentor provides guidance.
- A team provides guidance.
- A team provides a place.
- Peers provide support.
- Others will pay attention.
- Others will follow or give allegiance or loyalty.
- Other?

Perhaps your primary role as parent to a person-motivated child will be to teach him to discern the positive from the negative in other people. Your child may tend to respond to outsiders without thinking through their influence on his life. Your carefully stated questions will help the child consider the implications of his involvement with others.

If your child is pulled into action by circumstances, which of the following conditions seem to influence him most strongly?

- There is opportunity to do better than someone else.
- A difficult task or feat beckons.
- Excellence can be demonstrated.
- Conflict can be engaged.
- Something can be collected.
- Money can be made.
- Abilities or skills can be developed.
- There is a possibility of winning.
- An adventure opens up.
- Something new can be built or developed.
- Changes can be made.
- Conflicts can be resolved.
- A discovery can be made.
- Order can be established.
- Some form of expression can take place.
- Performance is possible.
- Other?

Discussing your child's interests with him can help him become more aware of what motivates him. Giving him choices between activities will be important for his growth. As you discover what motivates him and create these conditions, you may find that your child is more responsive to you.

Discover Your Child's Speed

We all go through life at different speeds in response to our own inner clock. Some of us race through life as if tuned to an inner stop watch. Others of us plod through life carefully and methodically following an inner calendar more than a clock. Our children also have their own pace of life. In order to understand your child's uniqueness and adjust to his pace, you need to find out what kind of timepiece governs his behavior.

A child who operates by an inner stop watch doesn't waste much time. This child:

- likes to finish a task at one sitting.
- wants a project finished by the time the day is done.
- can produce a lot in a short period of time.
- likes immediate results and feedback.
- can do things spontaneously.

A child who has an "average" inner clock uses a moderate amount of time for tasks. This child:

- wants to take the "proper" amount of time.
- takes adequate time to complete a task.
- shows care and concern in performing a task.
- prefers short-range tasks and goals.

A child who is tuned to an inner calendar requires a lot of time to complete his tasks. This child:

- is careful and meticulous about his work.
- processes and thinks through details.
- cannot or will not allow himself to be rushed.
- enjoys being precise.

- is very thorough in covering every point.
- wants to enjoy everything completely.[3]

Discover Your Child's Learning Style

Think back to the days of your formal education for a moment. Do you remember that some of your teachers had the ability to catch your interest and stimulate you to work hard while others tended to put you to sleep? Part of the reason you responded differently to different teachers is your individual learning style. It's likely that the teachers who motivated you the most were cooperating with your particular learning style, while those who provoked your mind to wander failed to communicate with you in your learning language.

Everyone—including you and each of your children—perceives life primarily through three avenues: what we see, what we hear and what we feel. But in each of us, one perceiving apparatus—either seeing, hearing or feeling—is more dominant than the other two. Our dominant channel for perceiving life is the root of our learning style. Those who are seeing-oriented learn best with their eyes (visual aids, diagrams, reading, pictures, video presentations, etc.). I am a seeing-oriented person. Things just register better with me when I can see them. That's why I prefer speaking to groups of people in person rather than on the radio. It helps me when I can see my audience and read their nonverbal communication.

Those who are hearing-oriented learn best with their ears (lectures, audio tapes, oral instructions, listening, etc.). And those who are feeling-oriented learn best through intuitive perception (spiritual insight, inner sense, emotional impact, etc.).

Tuning to the Right Channel

If you have a hard time communicating with your children, it may be because you are not appealing to their dominant channel of perception and learning style. For example, you repeatedly tell your child to put his dirty clothes in the hamper. You can't understand why he persists in throwing them in his closet after so

---

When you discover your child's unique motivation, speed and learning style, don't try to change them. It won't work.

---

many verbal warnings. You even promise him a candy bar if he succeeds at hitting the hamper seven days in a row. But it's as if the child is deaf! In a sense, he may be. He may be seeing-oriented or feeling-oriented, so your verbal lectures and warnings don't get through to him as readily. You may not be speaking to him in the language he understands best.

The best way to resolve the problem is for you to translate your message into your child's learning language. If you don't know what his learning style is, try communicating in all three styles to see which one provokes the best response. He's not responding to your verbal instructions about putting his dirty clothes in the hamper, so try appealing to his visual sense. Tape a simple, colorful, hand-made poster to his bedroom door or bathroom mirror showing a hand dropping a dirty shirt into the hamper. Tape an empty candy bar wrapper to the poster too as a visual reminder of the promised reward.

Or try appealing to his feelings. Talk to him about the sense of accomplishment he will enjoy after seven successful days of putting his dirty clothes in the hamper. Tell him how good you feel when he responds to your instructions. Talk about the importance of pleasing God with obedience. Put smiley face stickers on the hamper or on his napkin at the dinner table when he succeeds.

With a little time and attentiveness on your part, you can discover the perceiving/learning style of each of your children. Listen to their terminology. The words they use may give you a clue. Children who say things like "I *see* what you mean" or "Let me *see* it, Mommy" may be seeing-oriented. Children who make comments like "*Tell* me again, Daddy" or "I *hear* what you're saying" may be hearing-oriented. And children who say "That story makes me *happy*" or "I *feel* bad when I disobey" may be feeling-oriented.

Note also how they respond to the words you use with them. Try some of the following messages to see if they help you communicate more clearly:

Seeing-oriented questions and statements:

- "Johnny, it *appears* to you . . ."
- "From what you said, Sally, you *see* it this way."
- "Jim, do you *see* it this way too?"
- "Ken, how do you *look* at this problem?"

Hearing-oriented questions and statements:

- "Johnny, I *hear* you saying . . ."
- "If I'm *hearing* you right, you're saying . . ."

- "How does this plan *sound* to you?"

Feeling-oriented questions and statements:
- "Johnny, it seems you are *feeling* that . . ."
- "Sally, you are saying that this makes you *feel*. . ."
- "Ken, do you *feel* that you have a handle on this problem?"

For additional information on the subject of speaking your child's learning language, see *How to Speak Your Spouse's Language* (Fleming H. Revell), by this author. The principles for husbands and wives in this book can easily be applied to other relationships.

A child's learning style has nothing to do with his early experiences or his parents' influence. He was created that way, and his learning style is an intrinsic part of his nature. All learning experiences are important for a child, but he will find his greatest success using the learning style he was born with. When you discover your child's unique motivation, speed and learning style, don't try to change them. It won't work. Utilize your child's unique traits, and encourage him in those directions. He will learn more, and your frustration level will diminish.

If you have more than one child, you have likely observed the differences in motivation, pace of life and learning style right in your own home. You may find it frustrating to have one child who is bold and quick while another is slow and hesitant. You may have one child who needs only the printed directions on the box and does not want any help whatsoever building a model. And you may have another child who is a "show me" child. When he doesn't know how to do something, he will come to you and ask you to demonstrate it. No matter how many times you tell him to figure it out or try it himself, he will resist you.

Perhaps the best way to sum up the importance of understanding each child's uniqueness is to quote one of my favorite writers, Chuck Swindoll:

> If parents were to ask me, "What is the greatest gift we could give our young child?" I would answer rather quickly: a sensitive spirit. That is especially rare among busy parents who live under the demand of hurried schedules, constantly doing battle with the tyranny of the urgent. Nevertheless, my counsel to you would be, give your child the time it takes to find out how he or she is put together. Help your child know who he or she is. Discuss those things with your children. Help them know themselves so that they learn to love and accept themselves as they are. Then, as they move into a society that seems committed to pounding them into another shape, they will remain true to themselves, secure in their independent walk with their God.[4]

FOR THOUGHT AND DISCUSSION

Share your responses with your spouse, a trusted friend or your study group.

1. Write the names of each of your children in the spaces below. Then write at least three descriptive words for each which highlight their uniqueness in your family (leader, computer nut, tidy, sweet tooth,

etc.). Try not to use the same word to describe more than one child.

• Name:
   1.
   2.
   3.

• Name:
   1.
   2.
   3.

• Name:
   1.
   2.
   3.

• Name:
   1.
   2.
   3.

2. How are each of your children unique in the categories of motivation, speed and learning style? Fill in their names below, then describe their uniqueness in each of the three categories in a few words.

• Name:
   Motivation:
   Speed:
   Learning style:

- Name:
  Motivation:
  Speed:
  Learning style:

- Name:
  Motivation:
  Speed:
  Learning style:

- Name:
  Motivation:
  Speed:
  Learning style:

Notes
1. Ralph Mattson and Thom Black, *Discovering Your Child's Design* (Elgin, IL: David C. Cook Publishers, 1989), adapted from pp. 61-64.
2. Ann Crittenden, "Babies Are Born Different," *McCall's* (September, 1986), adapted from pp. 107, 149, 150, 151. Quoted in Barbara Sullivan, *No Two Alike* (Old Tappan, NJ: Fleming H. Revell, 1987), p. 35. Used by permission.
3. Mattson and Black, *Discovering Your Child's Design*, adapted from pp. 108-112.
4. From the book *Growing Wise in Family Life* by Charles R. Swindoll, copyright 1988 by Charles R. Swindoll, Inc. Published by Multnomah Press, Portland, Oregon 97266. Used by permission.

10

GETTING THROUGH TO NUMBER ONE

WHY are some children dominant leaders while others are passive followers? Why do some tend to be neat and orderly while others are sloppy? What accounts for the seemingly infinite number of differences which exist from child to child? In short, what makes each child unique?

There are a number of hereditary and environmental factors which contribute to a child's uniqueness. In the next three chapters we will consider two of the most prominent: birth order and personality. In this chapter we will look at the unique characteristics of the firstborn child in the family, and in chapter 11 we will explore the traits of middle-born and last-born children. Human personality development in children has been explained and categorized a number of different ways over the years. In chapters 12 and 13 we will discuss the view which I consider to be the most accurate: the Myers-Briggs Type Indicator.

You may be wondering, "There are a number of good books out on birth order and personality. Why do these issues need to be discussed here?" Yes, there are some good resources available for understanding birth order and personality traits. But our focus in these chapters is helping you tailor your communication to fit the unique birth order and personality traits of each of your children. Each of the chapters ahead will provide specific tips for responding verbally and nonverbally to each child.

LABELS ARE FOR THINGS, NOT PEOPLE

"Read the label."

"Look for the proper label."

"Without this certified label, you could be getting the wrong product."

We live in a world of labels. We check labels to make sure of the ingredient. We buy labels to make sure we are wearing what happens to be trendy. We look to a label to protect our health and our investment. Think with me for a minute. How many items did you wear or use today that had a label? Probably several.

If you went grocery shopping you were drawn to a number of items because of the label. Why? Consistency. You can count on each item with the same label being the same. This is generally true with everything—except children. We tend to use labels because they give us a sense of comfort. I've heard parents say, "Oh, my son is a_____. Everyone knows what they are like."

Before we go any farther, I must issue a caution. Often when we talk about different character traits we tend to start labeling ourselves and others. For example, many of my clients identify themselves as choleric, phlegmatic, melancholy or sanguine in personality type. Others tell me that their spouses are perfectionistic, impulsive, subjective, second born, extroverted, introverted, etc. They assume that by labeling themselves and their husband or wife they are helping me understand exactly what they are like.

We parents do the same thing. We often feel that finding a label for each child will help us explain—and sometimes predict—their behavior. Identifying a child's birth order and basic personality style does help us understand our children somewhat. But every child is unique. Regardless of the label we attach, each child has his own set of unique qualities. When we label a child according to his birth order or personality style, we tend to overgeneralize. We see him only through the filter of that label, overlooking the God-given qualities that sets apart one first-born from another, one introvert from another, etc.

Once you slap a label on your child you may also be surprised when your child responds contrary to your label (which he most certainly will at times!). Furthermore, if your child hears you repeatedly describe him to others as, for example, an extrovert, he may attempt to live up to your label instead of develop some of the quiet qualities God gave him. In these ways labeling can be harmful instead of helpful.

The labels we use in these chapters to describe birth order and personality traits are only for convenience. As you read about these traits, you may see your children fitting certain categories. But instead of pigeonholing them with hard and fast labels, be ready to say, "Generally speaking, my child is like . . ." This balanced response leaves room for your child's uniqueness.

You will probably identify yourself as well as your children in the descriptions ahead. It's good that you have an idea of your own unique blend of traits, since your personality will affect your expectations for your children. But don't be surprised if discover that you don't share the same traits as your children. That's where so much frustration in parent-child communication occurs. We sometimes expect our children to act like us and respond like us. We subconsciously label them with our own label. But remember: Your children are unique. They are not cookie-cutter replicas of each other or of you, and that's all right. That's how God made them.

THE FIRSTBORN

An individual's birth order in the family has a lifelong effect on who he is and what he turns out to be. Birth order helps make a child unique. Birth order combines with other elements such as personality, temperament and parental relationships to shape the child and determine the roles he will feel comfortable in as an adult. Birth order can also affect a child's self-image, response to authority and reaction to life's circumstances.

A Portrait of the Firstborn

Firstborns are quite easy to identify. They are often achievers in their chosen fields. They tend to be more highly motivated to achieve than their younger brothers and sisters. All seven astronauts in the original Mercury program were firstborns. Magazine and newspaper reporters tend to be firstborns. Since firstborns like structure and order, they tend to enter professions which are exacting.

Parents anticipate the first child's birth with anxiety and excitement. They learn parenting by "experimenting" on the first child. The firstborn bears the brunt of the parents' expectations and attempts at dis-

---

Firstborns tend to be serious, conscientious, critical, perfectionistic, loyal, self-reliant and goal-oriented.

---

cipline. Eager first-time parents want to parent better than anyone ever did before, and so the firstborn becomes the victim of their inexperience, high hopes and enthusiasm. Instead of letting their firstborn develop at his own pace, most parents work hard to see that he sits, stands, walks, talks and is potty trained at the "proper" age or even before. And research indicates that firstborns do indeed walk and talk earlier than their siblings. Is it any wonder that achievement becomes a way of life for this child?

Firstborns learn to value achievement more than people. Often this person grows up feeling he has to produce or else. Firstborns receive encouragement, prodding and coaching from parents and grandparents alike. Everyone over-parents the firstborn. Unlike his later brothers and sisters, the firstborn only has his parents as models of behavior, and he tends to imitate adult behavior more closely.

Firstborns tend to grow up fast, and they feel the pressure of the adults around them. Even firstborn girls are pressured to produce, and they often wind up in charge of their younger brothers and sisters. Mothers have been known to take advantage of firstborn daughters, pressing them into service early as baby-sitters, cooks and house-cleaners. It's not uncommon for a firstborn girl to earn labels like "the warden," "little mother" or "mother hen" from her siblings. When the firstborn grows up and moves out, does the pressure to produce vanish? No. He continues to put pressure on himself.

Firstborns tend to be serious, conscientious, critical, perfectionistic, loyal, self-reliant and goal-oriented. They have strong powers of concentration. They are list-makers. They believe in authority, and some tend to be legalistic. Don't expect firstborns to come up with many surprises; their behavior is fairly predictable. This doesn't mean, however, that every firstborn turns out identically. There are no clones.

In general, there are two basic types of firstborns: strong-willed and compliant. The strong-willed, aggressive firstborns can develop traits that mold them into hard drivers and high achievers with lofty expectations and a need to be at the top. Compliant firstborns strive to please others and are usually very reliable workers. They feast at the table of approval.

The firstborn child tends to be cautious about intimacy. He doesn't want to get too close to other people. The firstborn may have friends, but he will usually relate to them through projects and accomplishments instead of on a close emotional level. Firstborns have the capacity for intimacy, but it takes longer to develop in them than in others. Since so many firstborns grow up being pushed to achieve and produce, they fear that they won't measure up and that their parents and others won't approve of them. So don't be surprised if your older first-born child or teen approaches closeness with others in a cautious, step-wise manner. They will often test the waters of a relationship first to make sure the temperature is warm enough to go a little deeper.

What happens when a firstborn marries? If a first-born boy has younger brothers but no sisters, he will expect much from a woman without offering much in return. He may be very particular about what he wants in a wife, and he often has a difficult time selecting the person he wants to marry. If he marries a woman who is the eldest of sisters, sparks will fly in their marriage since neither of them have much experience relating to the opposite sex and both are used to being the leader. A leadership conflict could also arise between a firstborn man and a firstborn woman with younger brothers.

Many firstborn males tend to marry last-born women with older brothers. These marriages are often peaceful because they match a leader with a follow-er. If you find a firstborn man with younger sisters you have probably found a man who knows how to treat women well. They often tend to arrange their lives around the needs and desires of their women.[1]

How Firstborns Communicate

Let's consider the communication tendencies a first-born child exhibits. Firstborns focus on details. As your firstborn child interacts with you, expect to hear about everything he observes in people or things. Sometimes the firstborn provides too much verbal detail, and you may become lost, overwhelmed or frustrated trying to keep up with his description. You may ask the time, and he will tell you how the watch operates!

Detail and verbal description are very important to a firstborn. He is very literal in his interpretation of the words you use with him. He is often an expert when it comes to remembering and using details to make decisions. Some parents say that their firstborns are obnoxious at times because of their ability to recall and recite details.

The older a firstborn becomes, the more he tends to see emotions and feelings as irrational and inferior to thought and reason. So when communicating with you, he may discount his own feelings and yours. When you communicate with him in an emotional way, he will respond in an analytical way. He will try to connect your emotions to the events he thinks would logically bring them about. If he cannot find any reason for your feelings, he may try to change them.

For the firstborn, feelings must be reasonable and logical. If his feelings can help him reach a solution, then they are important to him. But if there is any chance that you will view him as weak, vulnerable or unproductive because of the feelings he displays, he will block the expression of those emotions. Or if he believes that you will disapprove of the expression of his feelings, he will hold them back. Why? His need to be right and be seen as right is much greater than his need to express his feelings. If you disapprove of him or his feelings, his communication becomes hampered. He may even distort events or omit information in order to present himself as efficient and productive. He needs to hear supportive, nonjudgmental statements from you which affirm his feelings, such as, "It's all right to be upset and feel disappointed because of your school problem. Thank you for sharing your feelings with me."

How to Communicate with Firstborns

Here are a number of practical guidelines for communicating with your firstborn child based on his general characteristics and needs.

1. Be direct and specific. When you talk with your firstborn, be sure your message is very explicit. Ask direct questions, and give specific answers. If you tend to cut to the bottom line and give only basic facts when you communicate, learn to amplify your comments to your firstborn. Fill your messages with facts, and give instructions in a step-by-step manner. Give your firstborn a logical explanation for what you are asking him to do. Use inductive reasoning. This is how he makes sense of his world. Don't be threatened when he keeps asking you questions. He is not challenging you; he simply needs to make sense of your request. I've seen a number of blended families where the new step-parent wasn't accustomed to dealing with the firstborn this way and couldn't understand the necessity for such an explanation. The step-parent's approach was, "Do it because I said so." You can imagine the resulting conflict.

Since this child tends to be very analytical, he will find implied messages difficult to understand. A statement like, "It sure would be nice if you would help out around the house sometime," is too vague. The only type of message which will register with a firstborn is, "I would appreciate it if you would take each piece of china out of the cupboard, dust them all, clean the shelves and then return each item to its proper place." Make your expectations clear and attainable, and reinforce his efforts with statements like, "You did a good job sweeping the patio and picking up the leaves. You listened to my instructions very well."

2. *Affirm him as a person.* Your firstborn needs to hear from you that he is important for who he is as well as for what he does. Use statements like, "I like you," "I love you," "You're wonderful," "You're a neat kid" and "I like you when you accomplish so much, and I like you when you're sitting quietly and reading." When he is assured that he is valued for who he is, the amount of approval he needs for his accomplishments begins to diminish.

Since this child can get bogged down with his attempts to achieve, remind him that he is just as valuable and productive when he does less than he thinks he should. This might come as a revelation to him. They need to hear again and again from both parents that they are loved, accepted and approved even when they are not productive. Sometimes we reinforce their tendency for overachieving by overemphasizing their performance. They need to hear that any contribution they make is important. Firstborns thrive on direct affirmation like this. But remember to make your comments very clear since your child may not pick up your indirect compliments.

3. *Encourage play and relaxation.* Since a firstborn's self-esteem is so wrapped up in achievement, he can become overly concerned when he is not accomplishing something. So it's important to give him plenty to do, but you must also teach him to play and relax. Also, if there are several children in the family, the firstborn is often given responsibility for caring for the younger children. Sometimes he will resent the additional work if he doesn't receive privileges commensurate with his effort. Your firstborn doesn't want to think his value is based on being a baby-sitter or housekeeper. A special treat or a "date" with Mom and Dad alone, along with plenty of direct verbal affirmation, will help him keep work and play in proper perspective.[2]

> Give your firstborn child plenty of verbal and nonverbal affection even though he may appear to be aloof.

Another way to ease the pressure for your achievement-oriented firstborn is to help him learn to enjoy the process of his endeavors as much as he enjoys the final product. Compliment him for successful steps and good attempts as much as for the end result. Help him understand when he has done enough. If he brings home a report card with all *A*'s and one *B*, don't focus on the *B*. Firstborns have perfectionistic tendencies anyway, and they need to be reminded to appreciate their efforts as well as their shining triumphs.

4. Compliment as you correct. When you must correct your first-born, he will be able to handle it better if you acknowledge his effort. If you begin by pointing out his mistake, he may fail to hear the rest of your message. So preface your correction with pos-

itive statements like "I understand what you were trying to do" or "Let's think about a different way you
could try this." If you correct with a harsh, disapproving tone, this child will hear only your tone, not your
message, and become defensive.

5. Help him explore and express his feelings.
When you find your firstborn bogged down in the
details of a project, help him acknowledge and deal
with his feelings of helplessness, confusion and fear.
He needs permission to feel that way and to talk about
his feelings. But beware: Any hint of judgment or condemnation from you will put a damper on his feelings. Affirm his efforts on the project, but also convey
that you understand the frustration he is experiencing
in his complicated problem.

Show him the connection between feelings and
facts. Remember: Firstborns need good reasons (from
their perspective) for their feelings. Help your child
by reflecting how you think he feels. For example,
you may say something like, "John, I see two reasons
why you and I both are disappointed about our trip
being cancelled. They are..."

Because the firstborn struggles to express his feelings, it is important to give explicit praise and affirmation whenever he shares his feelings, relates personal information or expresses affection. Your affirmation will help him become more confident about
revealing himself and less afraid of closeness with others. He will discover, "I can do this correctly too!" He
will be greatly relieved when he discovers that others
can understand the struggle he has with feeling inad-
equate. He will also begin to discover that it's all right
to be less than perfect.

Give your firstborn child plenty of verbal and nonverbal affection even though he may appear to be aloof. He needs to be touched and told about your love as much as any other child.

Do you have the characteristics of the child we have been discussing? If you manifest the tendencies of a firstborn, have you considered how this affects your style of parenting and responding to your children and spouse? Our personality tendencies can often get in the way of discovering the uniqueness of our children and relating to them as individuals. Clashing with your firstborn in birth order and personality traits can be the major source of frustration in the family. Accepting your differences and developing flexibility in relating to your children will take time, but it is possible. Allow your firstborn child to be the person God designed him to be. As you do, you will assist Him in the process of your child's growth and development.[3]

FOR THOUGHT AND DISCUSSION

Share your responses with your spouse, a trusted friend or your study group.

1. Who was the firstborn in your family of origin, you or an older brother or sister? How does he/she match the portrait of the firstborn in this chapter? How is he/she different from the portrait?

2. How does your firstborn child match the portrait in this chapter? How is he/she different from the portrait?

3. How would you rate your success at communicat-

ing with your firstborn according to the five guidelines below? Circle the phrase which best summarizes your level of success for each:

- Be direct and specific

| Very successful | Moderately successful | Moderately unsuccessful | Very unsuccessful |

- Affirm him as a person

| Very successful | Moderately successful | Moderately unsuccessful | Very unsuccessful |

- Encourage play and relaxation

| Very successful | Moderately successful | Moderately unsuccessful | Very unsuccessful |

- Compliment as you correct

| Very successful | Moderately successful | Moderately unsuccessful | Very unsuccessful |

- Help him explore and express his feelings

| Very successful | Moderately successful | Moderately unsuccessful` | Very unsuccessful |

3. In the areas where you judged yourself to be unsuc-
cessful, what steps will you take to initiate success?

Notes
1. H. Norman Wright, *Understanding the Man in Your Life* (Dallas, Texas: WORD Incorporated, 1987), adapted from pp. 32-37.
2. Barbara Sullivan, *No Two Alike* (Old Tappan, NJ: Fleming H. Revell, 1987), adapted from p. 53.
3. Margaret M. Hoopes and James M. Harper, *Birth Order Roles and Sibling Patterns in Individual and Family Therapy* (Rockville, MD: Aspen Publishers, 1987), adapted from pp. 44,45,108,109,116,172.

11

COMMUNICATING WITH THE REST OF THE TRIBE

JUGGLERS amaze me! They appear so relaxed and confident as they begin juggling a few balls or pins. Soon they add other items which fly smoothly from hand to hand. Experienced jugglers are not content to keep the pins or balls moving in front of them. Instead, they deftly juggle over their heads and behind their backs. And for master jugglers, balls and pins are only the beginning. They can juggle nearly any combination of items: apples, meat cleavers, fiery batons, etc. Amazing! How do they do it? Jugglers must have intense concentration, commitment and desire. They must learn the procedures, the moves, the timing and the coordination. Then they must hone their skills to perfection through countless hours of practice.

Any successful parent of more than one child qualifies as a master juggler. You need to employ the same disciplines of concentration, commitment and desire. You must learn the procedures, the moves, the timing and the coordination. And you must practice your parenting skills continuously.

Your parenting task would be simpler and less frustrating if all your children were the same—uniform and easy to juggle like a few balls or pins. But they're not the same; they're all different. In the last chapter we discovered that the firstborn has certain traits and characteristics and requires special parent-child communication skills. In this chapter we will look at the unique characteristics and communication needs associated with the second-born child (or middle-born children if there are two or more between first and last) and the last-born child. Once you get a handle on each child's unique birth-order traits, you will find it easier to keep family relationships operating smoothly.

THE SECOND-BORN

A second-born child is difficult to describe in generalities. When a second-born child comes into the family, his life-style is determined by his perception of the three persons who preceded him: mother, father and firstborn sibling. The second-born usually plays off of the firstborn, and often tends to be his opposite. As such he may end up as either an antagonist or a pleaser, a controller/manipulator or a victim/martyr, or easy going or hyperactive, depending on his response to his older brother or sister.

If a second child sees the firstborn as unbeatable, he may become discouraged and give up competing, or he may become rebellious and delinquent. If the second-born feels he can overtake the firstborn, watch out for the competition! Often a second-born tries to discover the weaknesses of the firstborn and compete with him in those areas.

Second-born or middle-born children tend not to have as many problems or hang-ups as firstborns. They are generally less fearful and anxious than firstborns. Studies show that middle children are more secretive than their older and younger siblings. Since they feel they don't receive as much attention as the others, they tend not to confide in others. Their desire to be tough and independent can lead to many problems when they fail to seek assistance from others when they need it.

Middle children like to have lots of friends outside the family, and often run with the pack. They are often more susceptible to influences such as peer pressure or temperament than others. The middle-born child is often the mediator in the family. Sometimes he's a maverick. He usually has the fewest photos in the family album because of the attention shown to the important firstborn and the last-born "baby" of the family.

Parents tend to "let up" on the second child, and he usually receives less time and attention than the firstborn. This may appear to him as rejection. As a result, middle children become tenacious adults because they are used to being treated "unfairly." Their expectations are generally lower than other adults, so they are more accepting in relationships. Middle-borns are not as driven as firstborns, but neither are they as compulsive. Middle-borns tend to stay married longer than first- or last-borns. They feel that they didn't fit in too well with their original family, so they are determined to make their new family work.

A Second-born in the Family

Jamie is a typical second-born who functions as the family plumber. Even if everyone appears to be handling the stress and pressure of family life well, she is sensitive to and disturbed by any negative undercurrents of hurt, fear, sadness or anger in family life. She is aware of the discrepancies between how people act and how they feel. She is able to pick up subtle messages which often go unnoticed by others. She tends to take on the feelings of those around her to the point that it is difficult for her to identify her own feelings.

Jamie feels responsible to unclog any lines of family communication blocked by problems or negative feelings. How does she do it? A number of ways. Jamie may try to distract family members away from the problem. She may joke and tease about them. She may display the hidden feelings herself, act them out or even force others to clarify their feelings. She doesn't like implicit messages. She wants everything out in the open and dealt with.

Sometimes when Jamie sees other family members violating family rules, she takes it upon herself to call them back to order. This tendency sometimes put her at odds with her siblings. She acts this way for one of three reasons: typical sibling rivalry with her in the middle, a power struggle with the firstborn or another attempt to do her job as family plumber by settling conflicts.

Because she is in the middle, Jamie sometimes has a problem knowing her proper place in the family. She may ask inappropriate questions, give too much information or get too close to another family member emotionally or physically. Sometimes new environments are difficult for Jamie, even those that are similar to the one she's accustomed to. If she changes schools, she feels at odds until she's found her new room, met her new teacher and organized her new desk.

Since firstborns and last-borns tend to get the most attention, your middle-born needs to feel that he is an important part of the family.

When Jamie interacts with others she is usually tender, sensitive and caring, often responding with intuition and deep feelings. Because she is so sensitive to others, she is usually a good listener. At other times she is more rational and goal-oriented, focusing more on the task to be accomplished than anyone's feelings. In fact, there are some days when Jamie is so emotionally distant, everyone else feels totally shut out. Yet Jamie isn't even aware that she has done this. And because it really wasn't her intention, she doesn't accept any responsibility for it. This frustrates others when they confront her.[1]

Responding to the Second-born in Your Family
If you have a second-born in your family, your verbal and nonverbal interaction with him will be different than with your firstborn. The following guidelines will

help you improve parent-child communication with your second-born or middle-borns.

1. Clarify your feelings. In order to reduce confusion or insecurity in your second-born, be consistently open about your inner struggles and emotions. If you are upset, angry or fearful about something, your second-born will likely perceive it, so you might as well talk about it to reduce his stress level.

2. Be affectionate. Since firstborns and last-borns tend to get the most attention, your middle-born needs to feel that he is an important part of the family. Assure him of your love through words and actions of affection. If he must share something with another child, such as a room, make sure that he has some area of the house or a significant object he can call his own.

Since your second-born may have difficulty expressing emotions, you will need to talk with him about how, when and where to give and receive affection appropriately.

3. Provide emotional stability. When your second-born is emotionally upset, reassure him that he is loved and important to you. Try not to react emotionally. If you become upset, he may adopt your feelings as well, further complicating the issue. Instead, respond lovingly and rationally. Hold him and say, "Later, when you have calmed down and feel better, we can talk about it."

When the child is able to talk, ask him what he is feeling. Help him separate his emotions from those of other people involved in the problem. You might even ask something like, "Is this your own feeling, or are you just expressing what your sister is feeling?"

When a second-born feels threatened, he tends to behave in an obnoxious way: throwing a tantrum, hitting, yelling, name-calling, etc. His reaction often provokes rejection from others, which is understandable. At these times he needs calm words of assurance from you about his place in the family and your love for him. Your emotional stability will pave the way for a discussion of the consequences of his obnoxious behavior.

4. Encourage communication, but don't demand it. If your second-born assumes he has told you all about what he thinks or feels, but hasn't, don't berate him or criticize him for his lack of sharing. Just ask him if there is something he has forgotten to mention. If you simply express your interest in hearing more, he will feel better about sharing more with you.

By the same token, don't inundate your second-born with your communication. Find out how much he needs to know, provide the necessary information and avoid long explanations.

5. Learn to communicate visually. Second-borns tend to think and learn visually. Communicate to your second-born in ways he can see. When you speak to him, use metaphors which will prompt mental pictures for him. Also, encourage your child to express himself to you in visual terms. Asking him to tell you what he "sees" or to describe the picture in his mind will help him communicate better.

THE THIRD-BORN IN THE FAMILY

Third-born Danny entered a family in which relationships were already established. Remember what it was like when you moved as a child? You entered a new neighborhood and a new school and the other children already had their friends and relationships. It took awhile to break in and find your place. It's the same way with a "Dan" in a family. Mom and Dad weren't as excited about Danny's birth as they were about their first and second-born. In fact, family life was already so busy that Danny didn't receive much attention at first. It took him awhile to break in and find his place. He was accepted and loved, but he had fewer opportunities to develop one-on-one relationships in his family than his older siblings did.

As the fifth member of the family, Danny is often the fifth wheel in family activities and discussions, requiring greater effort from everyone to make sure that all members' needs are met. As Danny grows up, he tends to appoint himself to the task of maintaining balance between family members without playing favorites. He stands up for one person one time, then stands up for another person on another occasion. He is constantly balancing the scales so family members are in harmony with one another.

Danny is very comfortable with people, but he is cautious about developing deep relationships with others. He wants to know exactly where he stands with them first. He may detach himself from a close relationship so he doesn't feel trapped or confined. This sometimes confuses Danny's friends. One day he is warm, caring and involved, and the next day he is distant. He is inconsistent and contradictory in his relationships. But when his parents talk to him about it, he is surprised. He always thinks of himself as an involved and caring person.

Danny has learned to get attention by being the clown of the family. He can break up family tension by causing others to laugh. Since Dan is the "odd man out," he can become a very astute observer of human nature. He understands other people. He can use his humor to control situations and to avoid sharing his own thoughts or feelings of discomfort.

Like some third-borns, Danny is emotionally immature because he missed out on some close family relationships. As a result, he tends to be inward, visionary and idealistic. He daydreams and fantasize a lot. When Danny has a conflict with someone, he often withdraws to resolve the concern in his own mind. He tends to focus on the issues rather than on feelings. When he has it all worked out, he returns to the relationship and announces, "No problem; it's all resolved." This tactic often frustrates his friends because Danny leaves them and their feelings out of the process.

Emotionally, Dan feels deeply and is a sensitive, caring person. But he sometimes appears apathetic when he withdraws from being close to someone while he figures something out in his mind. This distancing is how third children maintain their own identity. Much of his identity and sense of being comfortable is based on how well others in the family get along. His self-esteem is very much based on the stability of his parents' marriage and how they feel about him. Often Dan wants to know how others feel about him. When he knows that both parents love and accept him regardless of what he does, he is comfortable.

Dan feels most secure when he knows how every part of the family relationships work and that they're in order. He really feels good when he can help others. He feels the worst when he doesn't have many choices or options open to him with other people. When choices are taken away he tends to rebel or withdraw. He likes to make choices on his own but his anger flares up when someone else forces him to choose. He doesn't like to be boxed in by others. It's not making the choice that is important to him, it's having the opportunity to make a choice. Sometimes he even wavers when it comes to making a decision.

This tendency affects his closeness with other people. He likes to wait and see if other people can be trusted. His family and friends often wonder, "Does Dan want a close relationship or not?" But Dan just doesn't want to be confined or have his choices taken away from him. He has two main fears—freedom and abandonment. He likes his freedom but is afraid that others won't like him or will get fed up with him and drop the relationship. Even when he withdraws from being close to a family member emotionally, he likes the person to come after him and reestablish the closeness. This assures him that he is lovable and worthwhile. But if the other person doesn't do this, Dan wonders if the person ever cared for him in the first place.[2]

Responding to the Third-born in the Family

Here are a number of suggestions to help you respond verbally and nonverbally to your last-born.

1. Communicate and model interaction. Since last-borns are somewhat emotionally immature, you need to clearly explain positive ways your child can interact with other people. Help him understand the importance of being positive in his relationships and listening to others without interrupting. Of course, it will help him to see these skills present in your relationships as well.

2. Be affectionate. Third-borns crave affection, but they are not always adept at initiating it. Affection from you helps your third-born feel included in the relationship that is most important to him: family. Make a point to spend some one-on-one time with this child so he feels as accepted and important as the other children.

3. Respond consistently. If your last-born seeks attention by being a clown, respond to him just as much when he doesn't use humor as when he does. Let him know that you notice him and accept him when he's serious and when he's humorous.

4. Provide and discuss choices. It is more crucial for a last-born child to have choices than for his older brothers and sisters. He will appreciate that you take time to explore his options with him. But be sure to explore the consequences of his rash choices to help him learn to curb his impulsiveness. Don't box him into a corner or force him to make a choice. This is when his anger and stubbornness come out. He will fight to keep his options open and really dig in his heels.

5. Allow your last-born freedom to interact or withdraw as he chooses. When he decides to withdraw, don't take it personally or feel rejected. This is just how he responds to life. He needs time alone to work things out in his own head. Then he's ready to go on. When he withdraws, let him know that you will be glad to talk when he is ready to do so. Be ready to say, "You might need to think this through on your own, and that's all right. When you want to talk, I'll be here and ready to listen." Clear messages like this are comforting to him.

His withdrawal is usually not an act of stubbornness, nor is he abandoning you. But if you respond to him in these ways, he may not want to talk to you when he is ready.

6. *Don't interpret his silence as uninvolvement.*
Keep in mind that even when your last-born appears
to be oblivious to what is going on, he is still tuned in.
You will be surprised at how much he absorbs when
you don't think he is involved. He's just quiet about it.
All he may need is for you to gently draw him out.

7. *Explain the family benefits of rules.* When
you explain a rule for behavior to your last-born, help
him see how the rule will benefit him *and* the entire
family. Since he is so concerned with family harmony
and balance, he will be more likely to respond to rules
which help the family function better. And since he
feels better when he has options, give him some
choices for how the rule can be followed.

8. *Be open about marriage difficulties.* If your
last-born senses that you and your spouse are having
problems, he may act out his pain and concern
through misbehavior, excessive withdrawal or aggression. He needs to know that his parents are aware of
the problems in their marriage and are working
toward resolving them.

9. *Pour on the affirmation.* Let your last-born
know how much you appreciate him just as he is.
When he hears that he is appreciated, he feels comfortable about being the person who keeps a balance
in family relationships. Constant affirmation helps him
feel that he is succeeding in his role in the family. Let
him know that he is loved by his family even when he
needs time to himself to think things through. When
you see him upset or feeling alone, remind him that
you are there for him. Assure your last-born that when
he wants help, you will supply it, and when he wants
solitude, you will leave him alone.

THE LAST-BORN

What is the last-born child, the baby of the family, like? The attitude of other family members toward this child will determine in large measure how he will turn out. If his parents and siblings treat him as the runt of the litter, he may suffer from low self-esteem. But if they encourage and affirm him, he will have a strong, healthy self-concept.

Assure your last-born that when he wants help, you will supply it, and when he wants solitude, you will leave him alone.

Last-borns tend to receive less discipline—especially from the father—than their older siblings, and they are usually spared much of the parental pressure to achieve which their brothers and sisters felt. They may end up being the "baby boss" in the family, manipulating others with their charm and ability to show off.

A last-born child is usually quite comfortable in social situations. He may grow up to be a people person, a good salesperson and a "clown." He may struggle with taking responsibility for himself, since his parents probably doted on him as the baby of the family. But what he cannot acquire through responsibility he will steal with his charm.

David in the Old Testament was a last-born. He was cheerful and optimistic as a teenager, and he confronted Goliath with confidence. He had a childlike faith that God would take care of him no matter how bad the situation became. Years later he committed murder and adultery. But after repenting and receiving God's forgiveness, David returned to the cheerful, optimistic frame of mind which is evident in so many of his psalms.

THE ONLY CHILD

What about the family with only one child? What traits mark the only child in a family?

The only child may display the characteristics of both the firstborn and the last-born. He is likely to be achievement-oriented, and he often has a high desire to please his parents. But he feels safe in his relationship with his parents because he doesn't have to fear being dethroned by younger brothers or sisters.

Many couples center their lives on their only child. As a result, many only children believe that the sole task of their parents is to serve them and their needs. This will create some problems for them as adults. Only children may grow up feeling that life should revolve around them. With no siblings to learn from, they may have difficulties developing social skills such as friendship and sharing. Since they haven't experienced much jealousy or competition in the family, they may have trouble handling these problems later in life. The loneliness and protective isolation of being an only child may also be a problem. Frequently only children must contend with a string of broken relationships throughout life.

How do you communicate with an only child? Since they often carry the characteristics of both a firstborn and a last-born, you may need to build your own set of guidelines from those two categories. It is important that you observe your only child carefully and tailor your communication style according to the traits he displays. Above all, discover his uniqueness and learn to speak his language.

In the two next chapters we will get another perspective of how children in the same family can be different from each other: personality style. As with birth order traits, each child's unique personality style calls for a special approach of parental communication and response. The following chapters will provide specific guidelines for communicating with your child according to his personality style.

FOR THOUGHT AND DISCUSSION

Share your responses with your spouse, a trusted friend or your study group.

1. On a scale of 0 (desperate improvement needed) to 10 (no improvement needed), rate your present success at implementing the guidelines for communicating with your second-born child (or middle-born children).

• Clarify your feelings

    0   1   2   3   4   5   6   7   8   9   10

• Be affectionate

    0   1   2   3   4   5   6   7   8   9   10

• Provide emotional stability

0   1   2   3   4   5   6   7   8   9   10

• Encourage communication, but don't demand it

0   1   2   3   4   5   6   7   8   9   10

• Learn to communicate visually

0   1   2   3   4   5   6   7   8   9   10

2. On a scale of 0 to 10, rate your present success at implementing the guidelines for communicating with your last-born child.

• Communicate and model interaction

0   1   2   3   4   5   6   7   8   9   10

• Be affectionate

0   1   2   3   4   5   6   7   8   9   10

• Respond consistently

0   1   2   3   4   5   6   7   8   9   10

• Provide and discuss choices

0   1   2   3   4   5   6   7   8   9   10

• Allow your last-born freedom to interact or withdraw

0   1   2   3   4   5   6   7   8   9   10

• Don't interpret his silence as uninvolvement

0   1   2   3   4   5   6   7   8   9   10

• Explain the family benefits of rules

0   1   2   3   4   5   6   7   8   9   10

• Be open about marriage difficulties

0   1   2   3   4   5   6   7   8   9   10

• Pour on the affirmation

0   1   2   3   4   5   6   7   8   9   10

3. If you have an only child, what guidelines from those given for firstborns and last-borns do you need to apply to your parent-child communication?

Notes

1. Margaret M. Hoopes and James M. Harper, *Birth Order Roles and Sibling Patterns in Individual and Family Therapy* (Rockville, MD: Aspen Publishers, 1987), adapted from pp. 46-50,109,110.
2. Ibid., adapted from pp. 61-67,111,117,118,151.

12

YOU'VE GOT PERSONALITY, PART ONE

THE television interviewer posed a question to an audience of parents: "What one characteristic about your child either puzzles you or drives you up the wall?" Here are a few of the wide variety of answers he received:

- "My daughter is a real space cadet. I sometimes wonder what she uses for a brain."
- "My son has a big mouth. He's loud and goes on and on."
- "I think my daughter is a hermit. I just can't understand why she's so quiet."
- "My son can get lost between his room and the kitchen, especially when I ask him to do something."

- "My daughter talks first and thinks later."
- "My kid is so picky. He'll ask me the time, and I'll say, 'Oh, around four o'clock.' Then he'll say, 'No, I want the exact time.' What a pain!"
- "My daughter is so absentminded. She seems to be thinking about too many things at the same time."
- "My daughter is way too sensitive. She always gets her feelings hurt."
- "I wonder if my son has any feelings. He always has to be right, even when it makes his friends not like him. But he doesn't seem to care."
- "My son is only seven. But even now he has a place for everything and isn't satisfied unless everything is in its place before he goes to bed at night. Me? I let everything lie where it falls. But does he get after me about that!"
- "My teenage daughter is a procrastinator. She gets her work done eventually, but her last-minute antics disrupt the whole family."
- "I try to talk to my son, but he always changes the subject in the middle of the conversation. I sometimes wonder if his brain is stuck in neutral."

Do any of these answers sound like one you would have given to the same question? Are you itching to add your own answers describing a few frustrating characteristics your children exhibit?

Each of our children has quirks of behavior and personality that irritate us as parents at times. But in most cases the problem isn't that the child is bad; it's simply that his responses and thought patterns are different from ours. You get frustrated because you can't understand why your child isn't more like you. Trying to change his personality to match yours is as pointless and futile as trying to change his physical features to make him look like you. The key to reducing your frustration over your child's quirks of behavior is to understand and accommodate his unique personality style.

Every child is predisposed toward certain personality characteristics. These leanings reflect his genetic inheritance, his birth order and his early environment. A child's personality traits direct his preferences for responding to life, much like his handedness directs his preferences for completing manual tasks. Just because he's right-handed doesn't mean he never uses his left hand. He may prefer his right hand strongly, rarely using his left. Or he may be more ambidextrous and use his left hand for several tasks. The more he practices his handedness preference, the more he relies on it with confidence. Similarly, the more a child responds in line with his personality predisposition, the stronger that style becomes in him.[1]

There are many ways to catalog personality differences. I believe one of the most accurate is the Myers-Briggs Type Indicator. The Myers-Briggs material has been very useful in helping husbands and wives identify personality traits in themselves, each other and their children. An understanding of your child's personality type will help you diminish your parental frustration and curb any destructive communication patterns which may have resulted from your frustration.

The Myers-Briggs Type Indicator identifies four sets of contrasting personality traits: extrovert and introvert, sensor and intuitive, thinker and feeler, judger and perceiver. According to Myers-Briggs, each person's personality is the sum of his preferences in each of these four categories. Furthermore, the intensity of an individual's preference in each category will affect his overall personality profile. For example, you may be a moderate extrovert while your spouse is a mild extrovert and your firstborn is an extreme extrovert. Thus there are 16 possible combinations of preferences, as listed below. But the shades of intensity for each individual trait create an infinite number of personality styles:

- extrovert/sensor/thinker/judger
- extrovert/sensor/thinker/perceiver
- extrovert/sensor/feeler/judger
- extrovert/sensor/feeler/perceiver
- extrovert/intuitive/thinker/judger
- extrovert/intuitive/thinker/perceiver
- extrovert/intuitive/feeler/judger
- extrovert/intuitive/feeler/perceiver
- introvert/sensor/thinker/judger
- introvert/sensor/thinker/perceiver
- introvert/sensor/feeler/judger
- introvert/sensor/feeler/perceiver
- introvert/intuitive/thinker/judger
- introvert/intuitive/thinker/perceiver
- introvert/intuitive/feeler/judger
- introvert/intuitive/feeler/perceiver

In this chapter we will examine the characteristics and communication guidelines for children who are extroverts, introverts, sensors and intuitives. In the following chapter we will do the same for thinkers, feelers, judgers and perceivers.

THE EXTROVERT AND THE INTROVERT

Karen the Extrovert

Even at 10 years of age, Karen is an outgoing, bubbly child. She knows a lot of children at school and in her neighborhood, and she wouldn't think of doing something without getting some of her friends involved. Her parents often say, "Why don't you just sit home

> If you fight your child's basic personality preference by trying to remake him in your own image, you will frustrate yourself and wound your child.

and play by yourself for awhile?" But being alone doesn't sound like much fun to Karen. Whenever her parents require her to be quiet, reflective and work by herself, Karen tends to procrastinate. She derives her stimulation from being involved with people and doing things.

Karen's parents are also concerned about her study habits. She often does her homework with the TV or radio on. "How can Karen get anything out of her homework with this kind of a distraction?" they wonder. But she seems to be able to handle interruptions and distractions and still complete her work.

Even though Karen is friendly with others, including adults, sometimes she tends to dominate people with her talking. She likes to discuss problems with her parents, siblings and friends right when they occur instead of putting them off. But she's not always the best listener. When she has a disagreement with another person, she talks louder and faster and always wants to say "just one more thing." Sometimes she's guilty of speaking out before she has thought through what she's going to say.

People usually know what Karen is thinking because she often talks to herself out loud. Her parents frequently say, "Karen, who are you talking to? Why don't you be quiet for a change? Give our ears a rest!" Even at school she is one of the first to raise her hand when the teacher asks a question. She may not know the answer at first, but in the process of talking about it, the answer often comes to her mind.[2] Extroverts outnumber introverts in our country by three to one.

Responding to the Extrovert
Karen's inherited and learned preference for interacting with the world is through the traits of an extrovert. How can you communicate positively with an extrovert child in your home? Your responses must be planned within the context of your child's other unique characteristics as discussed in previous chapters: birth order, learning style, inner clock, motivation, etc. This is always the first step no matter what you child's personality preferences may be. With this in mind, here are a few specific suggestions for responding to your extrovert:

1. Let your extrovert be an extrovert. This may be difficult for you, especially if you are more of an introvert yourself. But if you fight your child's basic personality preference by trying to remake him in your own image, you will frustrate yourself and wound your child. Make the adjustments you must to accommodate his preferences as an extrovert. For example, allow plenty of room in his schedule for family togetherness and activities with friends.

2. *Encourage his quiet side*. It's not healthy for your extrovert child to be immersed in relationships and activities every waking hour. Whether he realizes it or not, he needs a little time for quiet reflection to bring balance into his life. Your task is to make the quiet side of life as nonthreatening and interesting to him as possible so he can discover its benefits. The best way to expose him to quiet times is in small increments. Ask him to spend 15 minutes a day—instead of two hours—in a quiet activity alone. Give him some attractive options for this time: reading, listening to a story tape, playing with a special toy, etc.

3. *Encourage him to talk about his thoughts*. Take advantage of your extrovert's outgoing style to explore what is going on inside him. Ask him about his values, and help him talk through his guidelines for selecting and maintaining his many friends. Your questions will help him reach some conclusions he may otherwise ignore.

4. *Be a ready listener*. As you show interest in your child's relationships and activities, be more of a listener than a talker. Don't rush him; patiently allow him to talk through his ideas and problems. This may be difficult for you if you are an extrovert yourself. You may need to discipline yourself to ask questions and listen attentively instead of chiming in with your opinions. Give him plenty of time and attention, and you will be rewarded.[3]

John the Introvert
John is different from Karen in so many ways. He

loves to spend time playing by himself or reading in his room. He seems to thrive on peace and quiet. He has learned to concentrate quite well in most settings, since it isn't always easy for him to find the space and solitude that he wants. He's a good listener, so other kids and adults like him. But they also see John as shy, reserved and even reflective.

John has two close friends, but he doesn't like large groups very much. He enjoys group activities like church camp when his friends attend with him. But getting involved in a large group "alone" doesn't appeal to him very much. His parents wonder why John seems to be anti-social even with them. When he comes home from a group activity, instead of sharing with them what happened, he heads for his room. They don't understand that he needs peace and quiet to recharge his batteries which have been depleted by the stress of being with a lot of people. For a couple of years John had to share a room with his brother, and he didn't like that at all. He waited for the day that he could have a room all to himself again.

Sometimes it's difficult to get an immediate response out of John. He likes to say, "Let me think about it" or "I'll tell you later." This often frustrates his parents, especially his dad who is an extrovert. But John likes to rehearse what he's going to say in his head before he says it. When he does speak, John likes to share his thoughts and feelings without being interrupted. Sometimes he gets upset at his dad who tends to butt in and even finish some of his sentences for him.

Occasionally John's deliberateness works against him in school. Some of his teachers wonder if he's mentally slow. They unfairly compare him to the extroverts in class who have their hands in the air while the question is still being asked. But when all the students are asked to think about a problem for 30 seconds and then to respond, John's hand is one of the first to fly into the air. He's not slow by any means.

When John has a teacher who bases part of his grade on classroom participation, he's at a disadvantage. If he has a project at school or church which requires him to make a presentation to the group, he will put off preparing for it and actually doing it until he is forced into it. It doesn't do any good to admonish him by saying, "Just go ahead and speak up; you can do it." He is very uncomfortable in front of people.[4]

Responding to the Introvert

Keeping in mind the impact of birth order, learning style, inner clock and motivation on communication, here are a few suggestions for your interaction with your introvert child:

1. Let your introvert be an introvert. Affirm his personality style with statements of appreciation for his quietness, thoughtfulness, etc.

2. Encourage his active side. Offer plenty of assistance when he is preparing an up-front presentation, and encourage him in his selective large-group involvements. Support him when he faces a threatening group environment such as a new class on the first day of school. Walk him to school or to his new class the first few days. Reward him when he responsibly follows through with group involvements he would ordinarily shun.

3. Give him space. Introverted children often have a rich inner life. Your challenge is to tap into it to discover its abundance for his benefit and yours. But don't try to force yourself into his private space, or he will shut you out and lock the door.

When you talk with your introverted child, do so in a non-pressured environment. Don't be intense or loud in your conversation; it will turn him off. Use gentle, probing questions, and suggest that it's okay to think about his answers for awhile before responding. And when he's ready to speak, listen attentively without interrupting.

Show interest in his solitary activities. Remember: It takes a great deal of effort and energy for him to socialize. Give him plenty of warning ahead of time when company is coming for dinner, and allow him time for solitude afterward to recover.[5]

In our discussion so far we have seen that extroversion and introversion are based on the way a person prefers to interact with the world around him.

"But wait a minute, Norm. I know several children who are extroverts and they vary from each other. One is really disciplined and organized, but the other is scatter-brained. One of the introverted children I know is really a thinker, but the other lives off of her emotions. What's up? Why the difference?" Excellent question. There are variations between extroverts, and there are differences between introverted children as well. As we consider the next classification of differences, you will begin to see why we are all so unique.

THE SENSOR AND THE INTUITIVE

Frank the Sensor

Whether he is an extrovert or an introvert, each child receives information primarily through his physical senses or through his intuition. Frank is what Myers-Briggs calls a sensor. He is more affected by what he sees, hears, tastes, touches and smells than by what he feels or dreams. He is quite observant, pays attention to detail, keeps his mind on the task at hand and isn't very concerned about what's next. He doesn't spend much time fantasizing or indulging his imagination. He's into the practical and the tangible.

Frank thinks very literally, sometimes he will ask, "Are you serious, or are you joking?" He likes specific answers to specific questions. When you ask him for the time, he will tell you the exact time. When he asks you for the time and you respond, "It's almost time to go," he will become irritated because he wasn't told the exact time.

In school Frank likes to work with facts and figures rather than ideas or theories. He doesn't spend much time indulging his imagination and wonders why people like fantasy. It seems too unreal for him. He is frustrated by scenes that are not built on facts and reality. He really enjoys classes where he is able to apply step-by-step processes. He is easily frustrated when his teacher or parents fail to give him clear and detailed instructions. If they say, "Here's what I want you to start on; I'll give you the details later," he's uncomfortable.

When Frank must think about the future or about something intangible, he will tend to procrastinate. He would rather be involved in what is going on at the present time. Seventy percent of people are sensors.

Responding to the Sensor
If you want to gain and hold the attention of the sensor in your family:

1. Be factual and direct. If you want to get Frank's attention, be factual and direct. Let him know exactly what you are talking about as soon as you start talking. He prefers to communicate like it's a newspaper article on the front page of the paper. Have you ever noticed the structure of major front page articles? The first sentence gives you a factual summary of the article in capsule form, and the next three paragraphs go into greater detail. Don't ask a sensor to analyze or solve a problem—and don't share your feelings about it—before you give him a concrete description. The sensor wants the bottom line first.

2. Give step-by-step instructions. When you give your sensing child a task, tell him the why, when and how up front. Show him that what you are asking him to do makes sense, and back up your explanation with facts. Give assignments one step at a time, and he will follow you. If your communication style is tangential or runs around the barn a few times, you will have to work at condensing and being straightforward. If you don't, he will either become frustrated and impatient or tune you out.

3. Appreciate his penchant for details. Since your sensor thrives in an informative environment, give him access to what he appreciates. When you give Frank a task, tell him why, when and how. When he talks to you, don't be concerned about hidden messages. Listen to his facts and don't rush or interrupt him. If he goes into detail, stay with him. It may involve time on your part to supply him with data to soothe his curiosity. But your commitment to feed his need will result in his growth. Expose him to life that he can take in and thereby grow.

Tim the Intuitive

Tim is Frank's opposite. Whereas Frank prides himself on being practical, realistic and matter-of-fact, Tim wonders about possibilities and loves to contemplate what lies ahead. He is easily bored with the details of day-to-day life. When his parents or teachers ask for information, he gives very general answers instead of hard facts.

One day his father said to him, "Tim, I really wish you wouldn't always answer our questions with another question." You know what Tim's response was? "Is that bad?" This is typical of Intuitives. He often answers questions with questions. When people try to pin him down to specifics, he becomes irritated.

Tim enjoys entertaining himself with word games and mind-stretching puzzles. His parents and teachers see him as a bit absent-minded, but he just has a lot of things on his mind. He is always trying to figure out the meaning of an experience. When he gathers information, he tries to fit it all together into some meaningful pattern. Tim's parents have difficulty with his sense of timing. It's relative. He doesn't think that he is ever late unless the game, class, meal or Sunday School activity has started without him. If the group starts late and he arrives ten seconds before they start, then he thinks he wasn't late! How can you argue with that reasoning?

Tim is usually the one in the family who sees the cup as half full and loaded with possibilities, whereas sensors like Frank see it as half empty with much less potential. Tim doesn't like to hear "it just isn't possible." Although Tim may come up with some interesting ideas, he overlooks the practical realities of his schemes. He focuses on the end result and fails to take into consideration the reasons why it might not be possible. With his attention focused so much on the future, Tim sometimes ignores daily activities and responsibilities which need his attention. He often puts off projects which require him to bear down and take care of details.

Encourage and appreciate your child's ability to lift you out of familiar, comfortable routines into a world of possibilities and excitement.

When Frank the sensor is told to clean his room, you can consider it done. He will pick up each toy or piece of clothing on the floor and methodically put it in the closet or toy box where it belongs. But when Tim the intuitive is left to clean his room, he will pick up the first object and spend 20 minutes thinking about its potential! Tim's messy room becomes a world of possibilities. When his mother gives him more specific instructions like, "Put your books on the shelf, your toys in the box and your shirts in the drawer," he will do better, since the potential for imaginative distraction is reduced.[6]

Give a toy Noah's ark and animals to a sensing child like Frank, and he will probably learn the names of each animal, admire their colors and facial expressions, line them up neatly next to the ark and play games in which they enter the ark in matched pairs. But give the same toys to a group of intuitive children like Tim, and they may decide to play church with them, passing the ark around as a collection plate and dropping the animals in like coins. Later the ark may turn into a salad bowl and the elephants and tigers into tomatoes and olives.

People who prefer to gather information through intuition often pay scant attention to the here and now, the actual, the facts. Instead, they are tuned into the future, the possible, their inspirations.

Children like Tim are often seen as creative, innovative and imaginative. However, because they are always looking for better—or at least different—approaches, they may be restless or even discontented.[7]

Responding to the Intuitive

What can you do to communicate effectively with an intuitive child? Here are some suggestions:

1. Feed his imagination. Give your intuitive child materials to play with that will spark his creativity—modeling clay, art supplies, building blocks, cooking ingredients, musical instruments, etc.—and encourage him to go to it. Introduce him to fantasy in selected books, audio- and videotapes and TV programs. Encourage and appreciate your child's ability to lift you out of familiar, comfortable routines into a world of possibilities and excitement.

2. Involve him in problem-solving. If you want to get Tim's attention, give him an interesting possibility. When you have a family issue or a problem to discuss with your intuitive child, ask him to help you find the solution. Don't give him too many details all at once; he won't remember them, and you will need to repeat them again and again. The problem-solving process may take more time this way, but your thinking, creating, possibility-oriented child just may be God's instrument for finding the right solution. Don't fight the way God created Tim.

3. Listen between the lines. I heard one parent say about his intuitive child, "That kid walks around with his head in the clouds!" It's true; they do. That's where intuitives live and where they do their best work. Encourage your child to share what's going on in his head. When your intuitive child talks to you, don't take his words too literally. He may be speaking in "code," relating his creativity in terms and pictures that are clear to him but fuzzy to the uninitiated. Try to discover his real message by asking "Do you mean . . . ?" until he fills in all the blanks.

4. Clarify rules. When the intuitive disobeys, it may be because he doesn't perceive the importance of the rules. If they don't make sense to him, he may wonder why he has to obey them. Explore the possibilities with him of why the rule is necessary. If that doesn't work, you can say, "I can understand that this rule doesn't make sense to you. That's all right. But we all have to follow some rules and guidelines that seem unreasonable to us. I guess this is one of those rules for you. How do you think you'll be able to handle this now?"

You will probably get farther with this approach than by saying, "Don't question my rule. That's the way it is; you follow it now!"

5. Help with follow through. Don't be upset if your intuitive child doesn't follow through with his ideas. He likes to plan, but he's weak at following through. Assist your child in following through on the projects he initiates. Whenever he follows through as

he should, discover how he feels about it and reinforce his behaviors with affirmation.

Before we continue with additional personality
types in the next chapter, take a few minutes to think
about the extroverts, introverts, sensors and intuitives
in your family. Use the "For Thought and Discussion"
section below to help you identify these personality
traits in you and your children. Then discuss the implications of your personality preferences on your family communication.

FOR THOUGHT AND DISCUSSION

Share your responses with your spouse, a trusted
friend or your study group.

1. Circle the number which best represents the extro-
   vert/introvert personality style of each member of
   your family:

• You

Extrovert   Introvert

0   1   2   3   4   5   6   7   8   9   10

• Your spouse

Extrovert   Introvert

0   1   2   3   4   5   6   7   8   9   10

• Your firstborn

Extrovert   Introvert

0   1   2   3   4   5   6   7   8   9   10

- Your middle-born
  Extrovert   Introvert
  0   1   2   3   4   5   6   7   8   9   10

- Your middle-born
  Extrovert   Introvert
  0   1   2   3   4   5   6   7   8   9   10

- Your last-born
  Extrovert   Introvert
  0   1   2   3   4   5   6   7   8   9   10

2. Circle the number which best represents the sensor/intuitive personality style of each member of your family:

- You
  Sensor   Intuitive
  0   1   2   3   4   5   6   7   8   9   10

- Your spouse
  Sensor   Intuitive
  0   1   2   3   4   5   6   7   8   9   10

- Your firstborn
  Sensor   Intuitive
  0   1   2   3   4   5   6   7   8   9   10

- Your middle-born
  Sensor   Intuitive
  0   1   2   3   4   5   6   7   8   9   10

- Your middle-born

  Sensor   Intuitive

  0   1   2   3   4   5   6   7   8   9   10

- Your last-born

  Sensor   Intuitive

  0   1   2   3   4   5   6   7   8   9   10

3. What helpful generalizations can you make regarding your family communication based on what you know of the extrovert/introvert, sensor/intuitive styles of you, your spouse and your children?

Notes

1. Otto Kroeger and Janet M. Thueson, *Type Talk* (New York: Delacorte Press, 1988), adapted from pp. 10-11.
2. Ibid., adapted from pp. 33,83,93,145.
3. LaVonne Neff, *One of a Kind* (Portland, OR: Multnomah Press, 1988), adapted from pp. 48-49.
4. Kroeger and Thueson, *Type Talk*, adapted from pp. 33,83,93,145.
5. Neff, *One of a Kind*, adapted from pp. 48-49.
6. Kroeger and Thueson, *Type Talk*, adapted from pp. 67-69,83-84,94,161-162.
7. Neff, *One of a Kind*, adapted from pp. 34-35.

13

YOU'VE GOT PERSONALITY, PART TWO

DINNER was over and the two couples sat around the table laughing and working together on a large fairly complex jigsaw puzzle. For over an hour, they had been working on framing the outline for this thousand piece puzzle; now the actual picture was beginning to take shape in front of them.

"You know," one of the fathers said, "working on this puzzle and watching it finally begin to make sense reminds me of what Helen and I have been discovering with our three children. It's taken us years to begin to understand each one and how to respond to their differences. We've been taking the class on birth order and personality type and even though it's not over, we're beginning to look at our kids in a new way.

"I used to get so angry and frustrated because they didn't conform to the way I wanted them to be and so

I just increased the pressure. I'm beginning to discover why my way wasn't working. I tend to be fairly cut-and-dried about things. If I could do it this way, why couldn't they?

"Then I discovered that I was actually fighting God! What a thought! I was going against His design for my children. And you know...my frustration level is dropping as I understand them more. At first, I was a bit overwhelmed by the information until I discovered it was fairly simple. It's just like working on this puzzle. We still have a few pieces of the puzzle to put together with our children. But it's starting to come together."

Do you feel at all like this father? Many people do. Parenting is like putting all of the pieces together. So far we've considered the child who is an extrovert or an introvert and a sensor or an intuitive. Some children are very strong in their tendency, whereas some may even appear to be a blend. Then we have to face the combinations. Some extroverts may be sensors and some may be intuitives. An introvert may be a sensor or an intuitive.

At this point you may be thinking, "Now I've finally figured out those combinations and I can relax." Not yet. We still have two additional sets of combinations to consider, and then your puzzle is complete.

So far we've considered the personality traits of the extrovert, the introvert, the sensor and the intuitive from the Myers-Briggs Type Indicator. As you discovered in the exercise at the end of the last chapter, you, your spouse and each of your children have slightly different combinations of these preferences. For example, you may be a strong extrovert and a moderate intuitive, while your spouse is a moderate introvert and a strong sensor, and your firstborn is a moderate extrovert and a moderate sensor. The more you understand the combinations of personality preferences in your children, the better prepared you will be to nurture them.

But we're not finished with personality styles. There are other combinations to consider. In this chapter we will look at the thinker, the feeler, the judger and the perceiver. These preferences must be blended with the previous four to give us the full picture of personality styles.

THE THINKER AND THE FEELER

The sensor/intuitive contrast defines how we receive information. The thinker/feeler contrast defines how we make decisions with the information we have gathered. Thinkers make decisions based on their logical analysis of facts and principles. Feelers are largely influenced in their decisions by emotions. Approximately 65 percent of all men are thinkers, preferring to understand their feelings rather than experience them. By contrast, 65 percent of all women are feelers.

No one—male or female—is 100 percent thinker or feeler. We all employ our minds and our emotions to some degree in decision-making. The thinker/feeler contrast simply identifies the preference each of us has in one direction or another.

Tony the Thinker
When 10-year-old Tony interacts with others, he wants to know the absolute truth about something. He needs to know the facts to his decisions. He tends to be skeptical until something is proven to him. When his parents instruct him to do something "because I said

so," Tony's response is, "Why?" He is only satisfied when his parents inform him of the consequences of complying with or ignoring their instructions. He is happiest when he can organize and analyze the facts before making a choice.

Tony enjoys hobbies and projects that relate to logic and science. He would rather work on a model airplane than socialize with other kids. He's more comfortable with tangible things than with people.

When Tony converses, he doesn't waste words. He expresses himself briefly and to the point. When his sister starts to ramble about something, you can see his impatience build. When people around him are upset, Tony stays cool, calm and objective. He wonders why others get so emotional over things that don't seem to have any bearing on the problem they are facing. If he disagrees with someone, Tony will speak up about it instead of remaining silent to prevent feelings from getting hurt. Thinkers would rather settle differences of opinion based on what is fair than on what will make people happy.

Tony's parents are concerned because their son seems cold and uncaring. Tony does care. It's just that honesty and fairness are very important to him. He even told his parents that it was more important to him to be right than to be liked by his friends. Tony may have difficulty as an adult understanding and expressing the feelings he has, which is the dilemma of many men who are strong thinkers.

Responding to the Thinker

Here are several suggestions to guide you in communicating effectively with the child in your home who is a thinker:

1. Explain yourself clearly, logically and concisely. When you want to get a thinker's attention, be sure to give him "the truth, the whole truth and nothing but the truth." No matter how you feel about the issue, you must present a precise, logical, factual case if your thinker is going to understand it and act on it. Rambling explanations or emotional pleas won't get too far with him.

When you ask your thinker to do a chore, he may irritate you by wanting to know why it needs to be done. If you have a reason, tell him. This will entail patience and thought on your part, but it works. In your own mind, you may be thinking, "Why in the world do I always have to give this child reasons? When I was his age and my parents told me to do something, I just did it or I knew what I would get! If it was good enough for me, why isn't it good enough for Tony?" You may be able to coerce him into complying without giving an explanation by angrily threatening, "Do it or else!" But that won't do much for your relationship, nor will it accommodate your child's uniqueness. He's inquisitive because God made him a thinker. Patiently and clearly explain your reasoning, or assure him that you will fill him in later.

2. Listen for his logic. When your thinker is talking to you, tune in to his logic and latch on to his main ideas. Listen carefully, because he won't beat around the bush; he'll get right to the point. Don't be offended if he seems to overlook your feelings in the matter. Remember: It's important to him to be right, even at the expense of your feelings. When his reasoning is clear and correct, accept it and affirm him— especially if you must swallow your feelings and admit, "This time you're right, and I'm wrong."

By the same token, you need not be overly concerned about hurting his feelings. If you disagree with
him, he will accept your argument with no hard feelings if it's clear and logical.

Whenever possible, ask your thinker for his suggestions or advice on a problem where logic and
analysis are needed. Encourage him in the areas of
math, science, logic games, computer activities, etc.
He can be very helpful in times of family decision-
making if you tap into his strength and affirm his contributions.

3. Encourage his feeling side. It is vital for balance in your thinker's life that you help him recognize
and accept his feelings and the feelings of others. This
is especially true of a boy in his relationships with the
predominantly feeling-oriented girls in his life.

Here is what one parent said to encourage the feeling side of his thinking child:

> I like the way you are so logical and factual.
> You've really developed that side of your life. I
> wonder if you've ever considered developing the
> other side of your life as well. There are many
> good benefits from knowing how to express your
> feelings to others.
>
> First, feelings are actually a source of energy.
> When you are aware of how you feel about some-
> thing, it can actually motivate you to do a better
> job. Sometimes when you are thinking about
> something, you may want to stop and ask yourself
> how you feel about it.
>
> Second, when you share your feelings either in
> person or on paper, it helps to get rid of stress and
> tension in your life.

Third, some kids respond more to feelings than facts. If you share your feelings, they will listen to you more often, like you better and be willing to consider what you suggest to them.

Fourth, when you're disappointed and hurt, you'll actually feel better if you admit your inner

---

Too many feeling-oriented children end up hurting themselves or becoming victims when they try to help others.

---

pain and talk it over with someone. Burying those feelings is like burying a lighted stick of dynamite inside you. Some day they may explode when you least expect it.

Finally, believe it or not, many of the girls you know like to talk about feelings. If you learn to talk about your feelings with them, they will respond to you more positively.

Heather the Feeler

Twelve-year-old Heather's decision-making is heavily influenced by her personal values, ideals, feelings and needs. Unlike Tony, who approaches information objectively, Heather interprets life's events subjectively.

Heather is very interested in people liking her and one another. Gaining someone's approval is often more important to her than being straightforward or even telling the truth. Keeping the peace in relationships is a high priority for Heather. She craves the appreciation of others and needs to know that she is liked. When her teacher praises her, she really puts out the work.

Whenever a decision has to be made, Heather is sure to consider the feelings of others. She could best be described as tenderhearted, merciful, harmonious and concerned for others. Even at her young age Heather is starting to put herself in other people's shoes. As she grows older, her decisions will be dominated by how she thinks they will affect other people. Sometimes she goes too far in meeting other people's needs, pleasing others to her own detriment. If she fails to balance her feelings by cultivating her thinking side, other people will continually take advantage of her.

Heather's parents are concerned about her being wishy-washy. She will say one thing, but change her mind if someone else takes offense at it. She often takes things too personally. While thinkers tend to impose themselves on others, feelers like Heather sometimes are imposed upon. It would be good for her to learn to say no without feeling guilty.

Responding to the Feeler

How can you respond to the Heather in your family? Here are some ideas:

1. Provide plenty of verbal affirmation. Your feeling child continually needs to hear that you are pleased with him, especially when you disagree with him. When you correct a feeler, include affirmation for what he did that was good. For example, "It makes me happy that you and your little brother play together. But today you were a little too rough, so you must go to your room." And when you want to see progress, just show genuine interest in what your feeler is doing, and he will shine to please you.

2. Encourage his thinking side. Too many feeling-oriented children end up hurting themselves or becoming victims when they try to help others. Give practical suggestions showing how your feeler can share his qualities of tenderheartedness and mercy in ways which are as healthy for him as they are beneficial for others. Challenge him to think through the personal implications of his people-pleasing actions so that he isn't victimized in the process.

3. Communicate in feeling language. When your child shares his feelings with you, don't respond with a lot of facts. Communicate first to the level of his feelings. For example, if he says, "I'm worried about the spelling test tomorrow," don't jump in with, "Give me your list of words and I'll start quizzing you." He may need your help eventually, but respond first with a statement like, "Thinking about your spelling test has upset you. I can see your concern in your eyes. It will sure be wonderful when the test is over, won't it?" Once you've connected with your feeler in his language, he may be open to practicing his words with you.

To motivate a feeler, share both the task you want him to accomplish and your feelings about his compliance. One mother said, "I used to make a list of specific tasks I wanted my daughter to do, and sometimes I would give reasons. But it didn't seem to work. So I started telling her how I would feel about her doing it as well as how she might feel about herself for completing the jobs. What a difference!"[1]

THE JUDGER AND THE PERCEIVER

Fred the Judger

Active, 14-year-old Fred is what Myers-Briggs classifies as a judger. This label has nothing to do with being judgmental or critical. Rather, it signifies someone who lives life by the rules. Fred likes to be in control. He is decisive and deliberate in his actions. His work and play are planned, scheduled and structured. He is so time-conscious that he seems to have a built-in clock. He knows what time it is, he's always on time and he expects others to be on time as well.

When Fred wakes up in the morning, his day holds few surprises. He schedules each day well in advance. He is upset when his schedule is disrupted by some unexpected event. He likes things done efficiently and purposefully. He feels that life would be a lot better if everyone around him would just do what they are supposed to do.

Fred is one of those rare teens whose room is fairly neat and orderly most of the time. He has a system for arranging his room, his tools and his books. He has a place for everything and doesn't rest until everything is in its place. He is a list maker, and he lets his parents know that his lists are important to him.

Fred is often emphatically and intensely opinionated. He sometimes states his convictions so strongly that his dad confronts him about his anger. But Fred doesn't see himself as angry; he's just convinced he's right. But he's not always right. He often jumps to faulty conclusions without checking out both sides of the issue or getting all the information. When he has a conflict with his sister, he tries to stay in control and seems unwilling to discuss alternatives. He also blames others when things go wrong.

Responding to the Judger

1. *Try to accommodate his time clock.* Your judging child feels more secure when his life is structured and predictable. Although you should not feel responsible to plan your complete family schedule around your child's time clock, do what you can to accommodate his need for structure. For example, agree with your child on a fairly predictable daily routine (e.g., wake at 7:00, breakfast at 7:45, leave for school at 8:15, play time at 4:00, supper at 5:30, chores and homework at 6:30, TV at 7:30, bedtime at 9:30). Stick by the schedule as closely as possible. When it must be altered, explain the change to your child in advance and negotiate a new schedule. For example, "Tomorrow after school I would like you to help me take the dog to the veterinarian. Would it be okay to move your play time to 6:30?"

2. *Encourage his spontaneous side.* Perhaps the easiest way to do this is to schedule some time for spontaneity in your child's life. For example, plan a family activity from 2:00 to 4:00 P.M. on a Saturday afternoon. When you all get in the car, announce that each child is responsible for choosing something for the family to do for a certain period of the time (go the park, go to the mall, etc.). This will give your structured child a taste of how much fun a spontaneous activity can be.

Cheryl the Perceiver

Cheryl is Fred's 13-year-old sister. She's on the opposite end of the scale from her brother the judger.

Cheryl is described as a perceiver. She is curious, flexible and adaptable. Cheryl thrives on surprises and spontaneity, and she is quite good at handling the unexpected. In fact, planning is a foreign word to her. She would rather let life "happen" than make too many confining plans. When it comes to school deadlines, she makes them, but only by last-minute, frantic, all-night study sessions which disrupt the rest of the family.

Fred says Cheryl is disorganized, but Cheryl doesn't see it that way at all. Her room is very different from Fred's. There is no order, and Cheryl likes it that way. She calls her room creative, whereas her parents call it chaotic.

Decisions require more effort for Cheryl because she feels she usually doesn't have enough information to make a commitment. Sometimes she waits too long to decide and loses some opportunities. She constantly looks for alternatives and says, "Let's look at all the options before deciding." She can change her mind again and again. You can imagine how this impacts Fred! But she is learning to be more decisive with the assistance of others.

Fred doesn't like to carry on lengthy conversations with Cheryl. Sometimes he comes into her room and says, "I have one minute, and I need a short, bottom-line answer." He does this because he has learned that Cheryl tends to drift off the subject in long conversations. She can be distracted by her own thoughts or by something occurring around her. That's why Fred calls her "Miss Space Cadet." Life is black and white to Fred, but it's all gray and intertwined to Cheryl.

Time is relative to Cheryl. Sometimes she's late because she was distracted, and sometimes she's early. One day she arrived at church for a youth meeting an hour early. So she went across the street to a store and ran into a friend. By the time they finished talking and Cheryl got back to church, she was 20 minutes late. That's the story of her life!

Responding to the Perceiver

1. Encourage his structured side. The perceiving child in your family needs the balance of some structure in his life, but he probably can't live under the kind of schedule Fred needs. Negotiate with your perceiver an acceptable schedule for some nonnegotiable activities (mealtimes, bedtimes, etc.). For example, instead of requiring him to be at the table for dinner precisely at 5:30, tell him to be home by 5:00 and you'll call him when dinner is on the table. Instead of strict times for rising and going to bed, allow a schedule with 30 minutes of built in cushion.

Help your perceiver meet the schedule by negotiating a reminder plan. Should you warn him? For example, when you must leave for church at 9:00 A.M., announce to your perceiver at 8:30, "We need to leave in about 30 minutes. Can you be ready?" And at 8:40 say, "Twenty minutes until we leave for church. You should be dressed and have your teeth brushed by now."

Or will it be best for him to create a reminder system of notes, cards stuck on his mirror, etc.? If you include your perceiver in the process of selecting a reminder system, he will be more apt to follow through.

2. Encourage his organization. Your perceiver may never have "a place for everything and everything in its place." But some guidelines should be set in place to cover your minimum expectations for non-negotiable tasks such as cleaning his room. You may say, "I don't care if the clothes in your dresser are folded or just wadded up and stuffed in the drawers. And you can decorate the walls of your room to your heart's content. But for the sake of health and economy, all food and dirty dishes must be out of your room before bedtime each night, and all dirty clothes must be in the hamper by Saturday morning so we can wash with full loads in the machine." Again, allowing a certain margin of comfort in the structure is the key to organizational guidelines.

3. Encourage decisiveness. Your perceiver needs to be reminded that he will probably never have all the information necessary to make the perfect decision every time. Some thought and planning is important, but eventually he must make a choice.

One way to encourage decisiveness is to help your child narrow his choices. For example, you take your daughter to the department store to shop for a sweater for school. Typically, she can't make up her mind. So after she has admired 10-12 different sweaters, you can say, "Here are four sweaters in our price range that you said you liked. Each style and color looked good on you. Choose one."[2]

PARENT TYPES VERSUS CHILD TYPES

Understanding your child's personality type is only half the challenge of learning how to relate to him in a nonfrustrating, nurturing way. You need to be aware of how your own personality preferences and expectations either blend or clash with those of your child. For example, if you are a perceiver, you may really enjoy the Fred in your life. This organized, capable child can get done what you never seem to get around to. But he may also be a source of frustration for you at times because he is often selfish and demanding, and his preference for regimentation and structure is a wet blanket on your desire for family spontaneity.

Be aware of how your own personality preferences and expectations either blend or clash with those of your child.

If you are a judger, you may really enjoy your Cheryl because she's so easy-going and unaffected by family upsets. But she may also drive you up the wall because you like neatness and order, and everything she touches turns to disarray.

Consider also the potential clash between parents and children who are thinkers and feelers. I've talked with a number of thinking-oriented fathers who have feeling-type sons. These dads are often frustrated because they don't understand why their sons are so illogical at times. They are also afraid their sons are too soft to survive in such a tough world. And some thinking fathers fear that their feeling sons are reflecting a weakness which is also present in their own lives.

Feeling-oriented sons have also shared with me their frustration over their fathers' lack of understanding. One young teen said, "I really enjoy art, and I think I have a future in it. But I don't get any encouragement from Dad about it. He wants me in sports. I like sports too, but not that much. I wish he could understand that I can't fulfill all his macho expectations for me."

I have also witnessed struggles between mothers who are feelers and daughters who are thinkers. These warm, spontaneous moms have difficulty relating to daughters who are so rigid and predictable. The mothers go through life wondering where they failed, while the daughters grow up wondering why they can't seem to please their moms.

Let's take a typical situation that occurs regularly in families—the use of the family car by a teenager. The car was promised to the teen early in the week for a weekend party, but the weather turned bad and started to affect the driving conditions.

Let's look at the thought processes of a thinking and a feeling parent. They may come to the same conclusion, but they take different routes getting there. The difference is the *process*, not the end result. Both parents care; both parents feel; both parents think. If they have learned to understand this about one another *and* about their teen, the resolution of the problem is much easier. But let's listen to the thinking of each parent. The key words which identify the thinker and the feeler have been italicized.

Arguments *for* Her Getting the Car:

Thinker: "We can each *learn a lesson* from this. Parenting involves *learning how to take risks* and growing up requires *learning how to take responsibility*. Parenting involves training yourself to let go, and this will be good practice for *letting go* when she is no longer under this roof. According to my *calculations*, the risks here are *outweighed* by the benefits of the *learning experience*."

Feeler: "How would I *feel* if the car was indiscriminately snatched out from under me without any regard for *my personal feelings?* She will *feel embarrassed* if she has to call her friends and ask for a ride when she was going to be one of the drivers. *If I were she* I would be *crushed* and understandably so. There is no way I could be so *insensitive*."

Arguments *Against* Her Getting the Car:

Thinker: "Parenting is a *tough role* and *difficult decisions* must be made. They are *not always decisions liked by everyone* and sometimes they lead to temporary unhappiness. However, *I am not called upon as a parent to be liked* or to make others happy. As a parent I must make *responsible decisions* that reflect a *competent role model* and that are *in the best interest* of everyone."

Feeler: *"I remember when I was a teenager,* one of the ways my parents told me they *loved* me was to *not always give* me what I wanted. Even though I felt *crushed and wounded* at the time, when I got over it, I really felt as though *they cared about me* enough to look out for my best interests. *The only loving thing to do* is not let her use the car."[3]

It may be difficult for you to discover a small child's dominant preference. You may see one tendency one time and then another at a different time. It's important to not make a decision too early that would restrict his or her development. A young child needs the richness of an environment which appeals to all of his senses and potential. He needs to have the opportunity to use all of the different functions.

Older children and teens may shift from their dominant function for a while to develop the other functions. Teens tend to shift gears anyway since their identity is in transition. Encourage them to explore new possibilities because this will help them achieve more of a balance in their lives. It will be important for them to both understand their own tendencies as well as understand and accept the differences in other people.

Minimizing Your Frustration over Personality Clashes

Some degree of personality tension and resulting frustration is likely in any parent-child relationship. Clashes between obviously different and contrasting personality types as illustrated above are to be expected. But even when a parent and child have the same basic personality type (e.g., both are extrovert/intuitive/feeler/judgers), they will differ because of birth order, inner clock, learning style, etc. And to whatever degree a parent and child differ, to that degree tension and frustration are possible.

How can you beat the frustration that comes with personality differences? Let me summarize the ideas in these chapters with three final suggestions:

1. Accept your child for who he is. I must emphasize: Let your extrovert be an extrovert; let your sensor be a sensor; let your thinker be a thinker. You can't change his basic personality type any more than you can change his birth order. Yes, your child needs discipline, balance and maturity as the person God made him. And God will use you to help your child develop his God-given tendencies. But you must begin by accepting your child's basic identity and by nurturing him through your words of acceptance and affirmation: "I thank God for you. You are unique. I appreciate your special qualities. I love you just the way you are."

You may be wondering, "My child is still quite small. How can I identify his personality type at such a young age?" It is difficult to discover a small child's dominant preferences. He will probably express many different and contrasting preferences in his early years. It is important not to label him too soon; doing so may restrict his development. A young child needs a rich environment that appeals to all of his senses and potential.

Older children and teens may shift away from their early dominant preferences as they transition into adulthood. As they grow, encourage them to explore new possibilities in order to achieve a balance in their lives. Also, help them learn to understand their personality tendencies and accept the personality differences in other people.

2. Adjust your expectations. Much of our frustration as parents results from unrealized expectations. A strong, athletic dad expects his son to be a star linebacker in high school. An outgoing, socially-involved mother expects her daughter to exhibit her social skills. When our kids don't live up to our expectations—and they certainly won't in all categories!—we become frustrated and feel like failures.

Don't allow yourself to get caught in that trap. God doesn't want your child to be exactly like you. As somebody has wisely said, "If two people are exactly alike, one of them isn't necessary." God created you to be you, but He created your child to be the unique individual he is. Don't require that your child grow up to be a perfect reflection of you (or opposite of you if you admire the opposite traits). Challenge him to be the best he can be at who he is. If you adjust your expectations to match God's, your frustration with your children will be greatly reduced.

Your godly expectations for your children should be reflected in your nurturing communication with them. Continually remind them of their God-given uniqueness and your desire to see Christ's likeness in their personality and life-style.

3. Pray for flexibility. When parent-child personalities clash in your home, you have greater responsibility and potential for flexibility than your children do. Yes, you must discipline them and train them to be responsible in the expression of their personalities. But you must also remain flexible enough to accommodate each child's unique personality type, especially when it differs from yours. A good daily prayer for parents is, "Lord, make me firm where I need to be firm and flexible where I need to be flexible."

If you would like to learn more about personality types and how they affect parent-child communication, I recommend that you read *Type Talk* (Delacorte Press), by Otto Kroeger and Janet M. Thuesen, and *One of a Kind* (Multnomah Press), by LaVonne Neff. Both of these resources discuss in greater depth the 16 combinations of Myers-Briggs personality types presented in the last two chapters. The more you understand your own personality type and those of your spouse and children, the better prepared you will be as a dispenser of positive, nurturing communication in your home.

FOR THOUGHT AND DISCUSSION

Share your responses with your spouse, a trusted friend or your study group.

1. Circle the number which best represents the thinker/feeler personality style of each member of your family:

• You
  Thinker   Feeler
  0   1   2   3   4   5   6   7   8   9   10

• Your spouse
  Thinker   Feeler
  0   1   2   3   4   5   6   7   8   9   10

• Your firstborn
  Thinker   Feeler
  0   1   2   3   4   5   6   7   8   9   10

• Your middle-born
  Thinker   Feeler
  0   1   2   3   4   5   6   7   8   9   10

• Your middle-born
  Thinker   Feeler
  0   1   2   3   4   5   6   7   8   9   10

• Your last-born
  Thinker   Feeler
  0   1   2   3   4   5   6   7   8   9   10

2. Circle the number which best represents the judger/ perceiver personality style of each member of your family:

- You
  Judger   Perceiver
  0   1   2   3   4   5   6   7   8   9   10

- Your spouse
  Judger   Perceiver
  0   1   2   3   4   5   6   7   8   9   10

- Your firstborn
  Judger   Perceiver
  0   1   2   3   4   5   6   7   8   9   10

- Your middle-born
  Judger   Perceiver
  0   1   2   3   4   5   6   7   8   9   10

- Your middle-born
  Judger   Perceiver
  0   1   2   3   4   5   6   7   8   9   10

- Your last-born
  Judger   Perceiver
  0   1   2   3   4   5   6   7   8   9   10

3. What helpful generalizations can you make regarding your family communication based on what you know of the thinker/feeler, judger/perceiver styles of you, your spouse and your children?

Notes

1. LaVonne Neff, *One of a Kind* (Portland, OR: Multnomah Press, 1988), adapted from pp. 35-36,70,93-94; Otto Kroeger and Janet M. Thuesen, *Type Talk* (New York: Delacorte Press, 1988), adapted from pp. 18-19.
2. Kroeger and Thuesen, *Type Talk,* adapted from pp. 71ff.
3. Kroeger and Thuesen, *Type Talk,* pp. 30,31.

CONCLUSION: A BRIEF REVIEW

I encourage you to keep moving steadily toward the satisfaction and fulfillment that comes from being a nurturing parent by applying the guidelines in this book. Perhaps you would be helped by a brief review of some of the most important steps:

- Tailor-make a blueprint for each child's character development. Be flexible, and remember that each child has his own free will.
- Give your child a legacy of love by empowering him to maturity. Help your child transfer his dependence from you to himself and then to God. This is real maturity!
- Identify the myths of parenting that may be contributing to your frustration as a parent. Identify and clarify your expectations for yourself and your child.
- Identify the roles that are developing in your child. If they are healthy, rejoice. If they are dysfunctional, a course correction may be needed.

- Put a permanent ban on the toxic verbal weapons of judging, belittling, blaming and fault-finding. Begin to employ nurturing communication which builds, supports and cares.
- Don't allow anger and frustration to trigger verbal abuse.
- Replace subtle, destructive, discounting messages with positive, affirming, nurturing messages. Learn to communicate verbally and nonverbally, "I love you for who you are."
- Discover the unique design and learning style of your child. Understand his birth-order characteristics and personality preferences. Affirm and encourage his uniqueness.

God has created each child to be a specially unique and fascinating individual. You have the opportunity to grow, change and learn to enjoy and nurture your child. As you do, the pieces of the puzzle will come together, and you will see your frustration as a parent melt away.